About the A

James Page-Roberts is the author of *Vines in your Garden* (Argus Books) and of the first-four editions of *The Best Wine Buys in the High Street* (Foulsham). He has also written around 800 articles on gardening and wine for magazines and newspapers.

Referred to in Punch as a Reformation man, he has behind him considerable experiences in life. These include farm labourer, prop-swinger, RAF pilot, medical and art student, matelot supernumerary, scene painter at Convent Garden Opera House, designer for the theatre and television, house designer and builder, world traveller, painter and sculptor, husband/father/child-minder/house-runner/cook, vineyard owner, photographer, sound and television broadcaster, and the subject of a Gardeners' World programme on BBC2.

He lives with his Dutch wife on the borders of Hammersmith and Chiswick in West London where he writes and grows vines.

The **Oldie** Cookbook

'Looks like we' re eating in again tonight'

by
James Page-Roberts

THE CARBERY PRESS

British Library Cataloguing in Publication Data

Page-Roberts, James
 Oldie Cookbook
 I. Title
 641.5

 ISBN 1-898470-00-6

First published in 1993 by The Carbery Press
Chilbolton, Stockbridge, Hampshire SO20 6BE

Printed in Great Britain by
HarperCollins Manufacturing, Glasgow

Acknowledgements

Thanks are due to the following for kindly providing illustrations:

Steven Appleby (pp. 34, 169, 170, 200)

Simon Cooper (pp. 29, 141)

Jon Cramer (pp. 134–5, 146, 149, 161, 183, 187, 194–5, 208–9)

Tony Husband (pp. 28, 62 136)

Kathryn Lamb (pp. 84, 92, 124, 153, 190)

Georgina Platt (pp. 36, 79, 97, 100, 108, 123, 126)

Geoff Thompson (p. 71)

Robert Thompson (title-page, pp. 24, 31, 46, 55, 151, 211)

Geoff Waterhouse (pp. 12, 16, 61, 119, 131, 155, 216)

John Watson (p. 56)

The illustrations on the following pages are by the author:

14, 44, 45, 54, 59, 65, 72, 74, 80, 85, 86, 106, 115, 121, 122, 125, 143, 162, 173, 177, 184, 202, 205

The publisher would also like to thank Antony Gray for his invaluable assistance in the production of this book.

Foreword

If my children are to be believed, I come from the last generation of men which has managed to live for over half a century without having the first idea about cooking.

First mother, then wife, then daughter have all cooked so splendidly that the impetus to acquire even the basics of culinary knowledge, let alone to experiment, has simply never been there. Cast adrift alone in a kitchen, my first instinct has been to head for the deep freeze and search for the fish fingers. If not available, a boiled egg has always sufficed.

For oldies like me, therefore, this cookbook does much to demystify the whole business. No complicated instructions, no impossible-to-get ingredients, no infuriatingly precise weights and measurements – all this endears me to James Page-Roberts' wonderfully simple (and cheap) recipes.

If, like me, you are impatient of detail, scornful of cooking fads such as *cuisine minceur*, *nouvelle*, et al., but enjoy good wholesome food, then this book is for you. I shall be giving a copy to my son-in-law this Christmas.

Richard Ingrams

Measurements and Temperatures

Precise measurements have been avoided where possible for the reasons stated opposite. However, where specific quantities have been thought necessary they have been supplied in traditional ounces and pounds, imperial pints and inches. Exceptions are made in the case of ingredients which are sold in cans or packets whose weight is measured in metric units, such as flour and canned tomatoes.

Quick conversion

Imperial	Metric	Imperial	Metric
¼ pt.	140 ml	½ oz.	14 g
½ pt.	275 ml	1 oz.	28 g
1 pt.	570 ml	2 oz.	56 g
		¼ lb.	112 g
		½ lb.	225 g
		1 lb.	450 g
		2 lb. 3 oz.	1 kg

Oven temperatures

Description	Fahrenheit	Centigrade	Gas
Very low to low	250 to 300	120 to 150	¼ to 2
Moderate to fairly hot	310 to 375	160 to 190	3 to 5
Hot to very hot	400 to 480	200 to 250	6 to 9

About the Book

Writers of recipes too often presume that those of us who cook at home have all the time and money in the world at our disposal. We haven't and we don't.

To feed and please spouse, children and guests, it is not necessary to spend a great deal of time on preparation or money on fancy ingredients.

With that in mind I have been writing this book on simple cooking for thirty-five years or more, recording the successful dishes with which I have fed myself, family and friends.

Here are some well-tried favourites compiled especially for men and women who, with children (or grandchildren) around them, run homes, pack a lot into life, love food and wine, yet are either unable or unwilling to devote much time to culinary matters.

Weighing ingredients takes up some of this time, needs more cleaning up and goes to preclude the element of chance – a matter that can make every dish a new excitement. My measurements of weight and volume are of a very general nature. They are only general indications so a certain amount of trial and error is necessary when you start. However, most recipes are so simple that failures will be rare.

The following dishes, being mostly of a healthy, 'country' persuasion, rely for their success on simplicity, value and taste, so expect flavour and satisfaction, not the flirtations with food of *nouvelle cuisine*.

The choice for vegetarians is wide when the vegetable dishes in the 'Hors d'œuvre' section are combined with those in 'Vegetables and Salads' and elsewhere.

Cooking in the following simple, forthright manner will, I hope, give great pleasure to you and those at your table.

James Page-Roberts

Hors d'œuvre

Starters and hors d'œuvre are the same. What both these descriptions imply, however, is that such dishes are only the lead-in to a meal. Those of us who have been brave enough to order one hors d'œuvre after another in a restaurant to make up an entire meal, know otherwise. Anyhow, many an hors d'œuvre, if served more generously, will become a handsome main course. This is the case with many of mine. They are dual dishes. Please consider them as such.

Green Bean Salad

Simple is beautiful.

Mix a vinaigrette (see p. 67) in a bowl.

Trim then boil French (string) beans for 5 minutes. As you are doing this, cut small chunks of unpeeled cucumber (about a third the quantity of beans) into the vinaigrette. Then add the cooked, strained beans to the vinaigrette and stir together. Serve immediately.

The combination of tastes, textures and temperatures is a winner.

YOU WILL NEED:

Green beans
Cucumber
Vinaigrette

Waterhouse

'I should never have goose – it always gives me gyp!'

A Mushroom Hors d'œuvre

The flavour and texture of cultivated mushrooms can easily get lost in many dishes. But they do make a wonderful hors d'œuvre. Having once eaten them raw at Philip Harben's house, I have since tended to use them as such, marinated, or only just heated through. Here are one or two of my favourite ways of presenting them as a first course.

Slice button mushrooms thinly (allow about 4 oz. per person), cutting them from dome to stem. Put aside.

Heat 3–4 tablespoons of olive oil in a large saucepan, add a bay leaf and about 1 tablespoon of wine vinegar. When you are able to sniff the steam without discomfort put in some crushed garlic. Cook this momentarily, then add the mushrooms, pepper and salt.

Turn the mushrooms around over the heat until they have absorbed the oil. Then, right away, well before they have started to shed their moisture, put them into a serving dish.

When cold, sprinkle a little olive oil over the top. Serve with a dusting of paprika or chopped parsley.

YOU WILL NEED:

Mushrooms	Vinegar
Olive oil	Pepper and salt
Bay leaf	Parsley or paprika
Garlic	

Mushroom and Green Pepper Salad

Heat around 2 tablespoons (if you want to measure it) of good olive oil in a frying pan. Throw in a thickly sliced green pepper and cook until soft. Add pepper, salt and a little vinegar. Cook a little longer.

Thinly slice about 1 lb. of mushrooms and add to the pepper. Stir around until the mushrooms have become quite coated by the oil. Transfer to a serving dish.

If you are eating immediately, dribble over a little extra virgin olive oil and garnish the salad with chopped coriander or parsley. If wanted later, pour off any juices that have been given off by the mushrooms (into soup or stock), adding oil and garnish at the last moment.

Serve this dish with hot French bread with which to sop up the juices.

YOU WILL NEED:

Olive oil
Green pepper
Mushrooms
Pepper and salt
Vinegar
Parsley or coriander
Hot bread

A Mustardy Mushroom Hors d'œuvre

Squeeze 3-4 garlic cloves into about 2 tablespoons of olive oil in a frying pan. Cook just a little, but don't brown the garlic. Stir in a pound or so of sliced, cultivated mushrooms (they will lose much of their bulk) and around a dozen black olives, stoned and chopped into bits. Add pepper and salt.

Turn the mushrooms and olive pieces around as they cook and become coated with the oil.

After a while, the mushrooms will quite suddenly give out some of their liquid content. Strain, and put the mushrooms and olives in a bowl. Return their liquor to the pan and add some vinegar and a teaspoon of Dijon or granular mustard.

Work this all together with a wooden spoon as the excess moisture evaporates over the heat. Continue until the mixture has the consistency of medium thick cream. Pour this sauce over the mushrooms and gently stir around until all the pieces are coated. Transfer to your serving dish.

Just before offering this delicious hors d'œuvre at the table, pour a little extra virgin olive oil over the mustardy mushrooms and cover them with a good dusting of milled pepper. Garnish with a few sprigs of parsley if you have any at hand.

YOU WILL NEED:

Garlic
Olive oil
Cultivated mushrooms
Black olives

Pepper and salt
Vinegar
Dijon or granular mustard
Parsley garnish (optional)

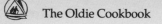

A Cumquat, Pepper and Mushroom Hors d'œuvre

This is an exotic and delicious hors d'œuvre, needing only a few of those little Brazil-nut-sized, cumquat oranges.

Boil 3 tablespoons of wine vinegar in a frying pan until only about half the quantity remains. Pour in around 3 tablespoons of good olive oil. Add a crushed clove of garlic and cook for a little.

De-seed a red pepper or two and cut the flesh into ½-inch strips. Add to the pan with pepper and salt. Cover and cook gently until the red pepper is soft.

Take off the lid and add a few cumquats sliced thinly (discard the pips that will jump out as you slice across the fruit). Cook for a little longer. Add thinly-sliced, firm white mushrooms, then switch off the heat. Stir the mushroom slices around until they have absorbed all the oil and become entirely (pink) coated.

Turn the mixture into a suitable serving dish and when cold, dribble over some more best olive oil. Serve with plenty of crusty bread (warm if possible) to absorb the delicious juices.

You will need:

Vinegar
Olive oil
Garlic
Red peppers
Pepper and salt
Cumquats
Mushrooms

Aubergine Halkidiki

The excellent tavernas in a small Halkidiki beach resort in Greece all served variations of this appetizer. The one developed at home was as good if not better than any indigenous version, and has become one of my most successful hors d'œuvre. It tastes best after a day's rest (in the refrigerator) so, if possible, make it the day before you need it.

For 4–6 people take a very large aubergine (eggplant), or several smaller ones. Score lengthwise in several places and bake slowly over charcoal to which you have added wood sticks – preferably dried vine canes. (If you are using a domed Weber barbecue with accurate draught control, place the twigs around the edge of the charcoal where they will smoulder.) Keep turning the aubergine until it is quite soft, chocolate coloured and almost half its original size. This method adds a most pleasant, smoky taste. Oven cooking will do perfectly well but the hint of smoke will be missing.

When the aubergine has cooled, cut it (with its skin) into smallish pieces. Put these into a hand-operated Mouli (using the disc with the largest holes) or an electric blender, add 6 oz. of crumbled, feta cheese and several peeled and chopped cloves of garlic. It will take very little time to work this mixture through a Mouli. If using a blender be careful not to produce a slime by liquidizing for too long. Season with salt and milled pepper, and gently stir in a little olive oil. Decorate with lemon slices and olives.

Serve with biscuits, pitta, or home-made bread (see p. 178), or just eat it with a fork. It also makes a good vegetable for a bland dish.

You will need:
Aubergine
Feta cheese
Garlic
Pepper and salt
Olives

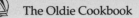

Yoghurt over Aubergine, Cucumber or Courgette

Cut a large aubergine (eggplant) into very thin slices (an electric slicer is ideal for this operation). Fry in plenty of hot oil until they turn golden brown on both sides. They will guzzle oil initially and give it out as they cook through. Drain, and allow them to cool on absorbent kitchen paper. Serve with yoghurt into which you have squeezed some garlic. This makes a good hors d'œuvre, vegetable dish or summer lunchtime treat.

There is a Bulgarian variant of this dish called Tickwitshki. For this one, fry slices of cucumber until much of the moisture has evaporated. Put the slices in a serving dish and cover with yoghurt to which you have added crushed garlic, chopped spring onion and dill.

The following is a cheap and successful version. Take a good-sized courgette (enough for 2 people) and slice it into thicknesses of about ¼ inch. Fry these in oil until they are brown on each side. Place in a serving dish, dab off excess oil with kitchen paper and cover with plain yoghurt. Dust a little paprika over the top and serve.

If you have more yoghurt than necessary, stir in plenty of freshly-chopped mint and mix with slices or chunks of cucumber.

YOU WILL NEED:

Aubergine, cucumber or courgette	Spring onion
Oil	Dill
Yoghurt	Paprika
Garlic	Mint

Aubergine Kefalonia

One of the great pleasures of foreign travel is to test local recipes and, if unable to find out exactly how they were cooked, to try to reproduce them at home with ingredients that are readily available. This one comes from a delightful Greek island in the Ionian Sea. It is a simple way to cook aubergines. The result is rich and filling and, surprisingly, the vegetable will not absorb oil with its usual thirst.

In a frying pan, cook a chopped onion or two in olive oil. As soon as the onion is golden brown and beginning to smell like fried onion, add water, some tomato purée, and/or chopped fresh or canned tomatoes, a dash of vinegar, a pinch of sugar, pepper and salt. Stir this around, then cut small aubergines in half lengthwise (allow half per person), put them in the pan skin side down and spoon over some of the sauce to coat.

Cover the pan and cook the aubergines slowly for about 20 minutes, adding water if necessary. Now turn the halved aubergines over and continue to cook for another 20 minutes, or until they are quite soft all through.

Lift them on to a serving dish or individual plates, cut side uppermost. It may be necessary to boil the sauce to reduce it to a thicker consistency before using it to coat the aubergine halves.

Serve hot, warm or cold. French bread to dip into the juices is almost essential.

You will need:

Aubergines
Olive oil
Onions
Tomato purée and/or fresh or canned tomatoes
Vinegar
Sugar
Pepper and salt

The Oldie Cookbook

Hot Cheese

Here is a spicy start to a meal that does not take long to prepare (well beforehand if wanted) and will take but a minute or two to cook just before you are about to be seated at the table. The recipe is roughly the equivalent of one enjoyed at beachside tavernas on the east coast of the Greek mainland.

Take 1–4 fresh chillies. Cut them through lengthwise and scrape out the seeds. Cut the green or red flesh into small pieces. (Be careful not to rub your eyes or touch sensitive parts of your body before the chilli juice has been quite eliminated from your fingers.) Peel and de-seed a medium to small tomato that is not yet fully ripe. Cut the flesh into small pieces.

Into a frying pan put a very little olive oil. Add crumbled, Greek or Bulgarian feta (sheep's) cheese, allowing about 4 oz. per

20

person, the chopped chilli and tomato. You may not need salt as the cheese will be salty, but mill over some black pepper.

The dish can stay like this in the frying pan until nearly ready to eat, then a low heat should be applied and the mixture stirred until the cheese melts.

Serve with hot bread, pitta bread, biscuits, toast or Melba toast. This hot cheese dish also makes a good dip when served with the usual variety of chips and crisps.

YOU WILL NEED:

Greek or Bulgarian feta cheese
Chillies
Tomato

Olive oil
Pepper and possibly salt

Chinese Asparagus

This is an hors d'œuvre equally good served hot or cold.

Wash thinnish fresh asparagus or sprue (thin grass-like asparagus spears) and snap it, from the head down, into 2-inch pieces – as soon as the stick bends and does not snap readily, stop. Discard the tough sections (use for flavouring soup or put them on the compost heap), and dry the asparagus.

Heat some oil in a frying pan. When the oil is hot, throw in some crushed garlic, some soy sauce and the asparagus. Cover the pan, lower the heat, and cook the asparagus for 5 minutes only, tossing the pan around and occasionally opening the lid to release steam. That's it.

This method of cooking what is really a very easy vegetable to grow, makes a wonderful change from the classic 15-minute boiled/steamed and buttered variety.

YOU WILL NEED:

Asparagus
Garlic

Oil
Soy sauce

Asparagussed Eggs

Here is a summery hors d'œuvre needing eggs and a few sticks of cooked asparagus – if you are strong-willed enough to hold some over.

With scissors or a sharp knife, cut off tender morsels from a few steamed asparagus stems. Now heat about 1 tablespoon of good oil of your choice in a frying pan and add salt and pepper. Gently lower in the asparagus to heat through, then break in some eggs (2 per person). Pierce the yolks and very gently stir around over a low heat until the whites are just set.

Slide the mixture on to a serving dish and sprinkle over a dusting of paprika.

You will need:

Tender, cooked asparagus
Oil
Salt and pepper
Eggs
Paprika

Avocados

Avocado pears are best bought when rock solid, and then allowed to ripen at home, unmolested by shoppers' heavy thumbs. My own preferences are those with hard, dark, crinkly skins. When they are cheap and plentiful, you may get a little tired of them served à la vinaigrette or stuffed with prawns. It is then time to consider presenting them with various imaginative fillings, such as the following:

Hummus; trout pâté; horseradish; a freshly-cut herb or herbs (mint is excellent); chopped hard-boiled eggs mixed with mayonnaise; cold, cooked (or raw if they are new and small) broad beans with mayonnaise; smoked cod's roe; caviar-type fish eggs – red or black; blue cheese dressing; grated carrot steeped in oil and lemon juice; oil, chilli sauce and chopped onion (a strong one, and chopped fresh chillies will make it stronger still). And on it goes.

Sometimes combine the additions with mayonnaise (home-made or bought). At other times mix with a vinaigrette as in the following 2 fillings:

Crispy bacon: fry small pieces of bacon to a crisp in olive oil and place in the avocado cavities. Add vinegar to the residual oil in the pan and boil so that it partially evaporates. Add this liquid to the bacon. Eat hot after milling over some black pepper (there may be enough salt already from the bacon).

Anchovies: pour the oil from a can of anchovies into a bowl. Cut the anchovies into small pieces. Work half a teaspoon of dry, English mustard and the same amount of icing sugar, with some pepper, into the oil. Do not add salt. Now add some vinegar – about ¼ of the volume. Incorporate the anchovy pieces. Stir well and distribute the filling evenly to the avocado cavities.

For stuffed avocados, extract the flesh from each half skin. Add finely chopped onion, pepper and lemon juice. Mash with a fork. Return the mixture to the skins and adorn. This blend is a stiff and excellent version of guacamole which you could serve in a bowl with taco chips.

YOU WILL NEED:
Avocado pears
A variety of ingredients

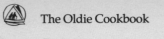
A Crispy Avocado Salad

'I'm sorry sir, you're a little late for worm'

Make a generous quantity of my standard vinaigrette (see p. 67), adding a level teaspoon of both dry English mustard and icing sugar.

Cut a ripe avocado pear in half (it's a lovely way of using up the rather insipid-tasting, smooth-skinned variety) and scoop out small pieces into the vinaigrette. Stir around gently, being careful not to mash them up. Now tear off small pieces of very crisp lettuce and add to the mixture. Gently mix everything together and serve.

YOU WILL NEED:

A ripe avocado
Olive oil
Vinegar
Pepper and salt

Dry English mustard
Icing sugar
Very crisp lettuce

Tomato Salad

This is one of the simplest and greatest hors d'œuvre invented. It is an everyday dish as well as being fit for any party.

Take some meaty tomatoes that are not absolutely ripe. Cut out and discard the hard pieces where they have joined the stem of the plant and slice across in fairly generous discs. Place these in a shallow serving dish or on individual plates and sprinkle with salt and a generous amount of ground white pepper.

Next, dribble over some wine or cider vinegar (whichever you like so long as it isn't flavoured), then dribble over some oil of your choice. Olive oil will provide a stronger flavour than that of say soy bean. Scatter a little finely chopped onion on top of the tomatoes. Finally dust over a little chopped parsley. That's all.

The tastes will marry if this salad is made a little while before you want to eat it – an advantage at a party.

Provide (warmed) French bread for dipping into the succulent juices.

The addition of slices of mozzarella cheese and/or slices of peeled avocado may make the salad more 'special', but it will no longer be the simple classic.

YOU WILL NEED:

Meaty tomatoes that are not completely ripe
Pepper and salt
Vinegar
Oil
Onion
Parsley

Stuffed Eggs and Egg Mayonnaise

Stuffed eggs are easy to make and provide an excellent dish for any occasion. Children like them, too. New-laid eggs will be almost impossible to shell, so make sure that they are a week or so old. One large egg per person is usually enough for a first course. But allow more for a light meal or buffet party dish.

Put the eggs in a saucepan and cover with cold water. Bring the water to the boil, then time the cooking for 10 minutes only – any longer and the edge of the yolk will darken. Peel the cooked eggs then cut them lengthwise. Extract the yolks and put these into a bowl. Leave the white halves, cavity uppermost, to await their filling.

Pepper and salt the yolks and mash them up with a fork. Now you will need a little moisture, and lots of imagination.

Softened butter or mayonnaise might well be your initial choice for this purpose. Other excellent additions include horseradish, anchovy essence, crispy bacon, curry powder, chilli powder and chopped herbs, fresh or dried. It will be essential to mix any dry ingredients with a little butter, mayonnaise, cream or soft cream cheese in order to provide a smooth filling.

Carefully fill the egg halves, piling the filling high as you will have increased the bulk. Finish off with a light sprinkling of paprika or chilli-con-carne powder and decorate with parsley.

For egg mayonnaise, boil the eggs as before, halve them lengthwise, place them yolk sides downward on a serving dish or on individual plates and coat with home-made mayonnaise (see p. 68). Decorate with a sprinkling of paprika and, if desired, leaves of tarragon or parsley. There can hardly be a simpler or more nutritious start to a meal.

YOU WILL NEED:

Eggs
Fillings various
Pepper and salt
Mayonnaise

A Curried Egg Hors d'œuvre

When on a visit to my 97-year-old mother, I asked her what she would like to eat. 'Curried eggs the way you do them,' she said.

This is it:

Heat some oil of your choice in a frying pan. Toss in some curry powder and salt. Cook for a short while, then break in the eggs (2 per person) and stir them around.

When the eggs are still soft and glistening (but with the whites opaque), tip them into a serving dish. Now trickle over a little best olive oil and sprinkle on some paprika, or chopped parsley, or other fresh herb of your choice. Serve hot or cold with toast.

There are other interesting variations, such as the addition of grated fresh ginger root with the curry powder, and grated cheese after adding the eggs.

YOU WILL NEED:

Oil
Curry powder
Salt
Eggs (2 per person)
Olive oil
Paprika or a fresh herb

27

A Smoky Mixed Hors d'œuvre

Fry chopped lean, smoked, streaky bacon rashers and slices of green pepper in some olive oil (say 6 rashers to 3 peppers). Add about a tablespoon of vinegar as you are doing this along with pepper and salt. When the green pepper has become soft and the power of the vinegar steamed away, turn off the heat and add thin slices of mushroom to the hot mixture. Stir the mushroom slices around until they have absorbed the oil and juices.

Allow to cool then place in a serving dish. Sprinkle a little fine olive oil over the top of this tasty and slightly smoky hors d'œuvre. Serve with warm bread.

YOU WILL NEED:

Olive oil
Smoked streaky bacon
Green peppers
Vinegar
Pepper and salt
Mushrooms

Broad Beans and Bacon

Here is an informal first course served with a jug of vinaigrette so that individuals can help themselves to the quantity of dressing desired.

Boil water and put in the broad beans, frozen or fresh. Return the water to a gentle boil and time the cooking for 5 minutes.

Cut thinly sliced, smoked, streaky bacon into small pieces. Fry until they are crisp, then rid them of excess oil by draining, then pressing them with kitchen paper.

Drain the cooked beans, arrange on individual plates, and garnish with the bacon pieces. Offer a jug of vinaigrette (see p. 67), leaving a spoon in the jug with which to blend the oil and vinegar. The bacon should always be hot – the beans hot or cold.

YOU WILL NEED:

Broad (fava) beans
Streaky, smoked bacon
Vinaigrette

*'I enjoy a bit of a challenge in the kitchen.
Today I've been grating Dairylea cheese'*

Hummus

This is one of those simple, economical dishes that makes a fine hors d'œuvre, a party dip with taco chips, or a light lunch. Children love it. It freezes perfectly.

For a good quantity, soak the contents of a 500 g packet (1 lb. approximately) of dried chick peas overnight. The next day, drain and put them in a saucepan, well cover with water and boil fast for 10 minutes then gently for an hour or two until they are soft. (Alternatively, to save time, you could use canned chick peas.) Strain off and conserve the cooking liquid. Process the cooked chick peas in a liquidizer, food processor or Mouli with its coarse disc.

Add half a jar of tahini – in actual fact you could substitute this with a lesser quantity of peanut butter which is cheaper, almost as good, and more readily available – stir together, adding some vegetable or olive oil and salt and pepper as you do so. It is at this stage (when the mixture is rather dry) that you can freeze the surplus in amounts deemed suitable.

For the dish itself, stir in lemon juice to taste, a little more oil if wanted, and some of the cooking liquor if the mixture has not yet attained the paste consistency required (to save carpet and clothes it should be thicker when offered with drinks). The addition of some pressed garlic at this stage is optional, but almost obligatory. Test for seasoning, remembering that it will take a while for the taste of garlic to permeate all through.

Stir the hummus and spoon it on to individual plates or into a serving dish. Decorate with black olives and serve with warmed Arab (pitta) bread.

You will need:

Chick peas	Garlic
Tahini or peanut butter	Pepper and salt
Oil	Black olives
Lemon juice	Arab (pitta) bread

Tuna and Beans

This is a simple, cheap and nutritious dish. Serve it as an hors d'œuvre or, in the summer months, as a main course with salad.

Soak your favourite dried beans overnight. (They could be haricots, red kidney, black-eye, chick peas, soy, etc.). Drain and put them in a saucepan. Cover with water and boil them fast for 10 minutes then slowly for ¾–2 hours until tender.

When cooked and still hot, carefully turn the beans in enough vinaigrette (see p. 67) to coat them generously, then allow to cool.

Arrange the beans in a circle on each individual plate and place, as it were into a nest, some drained and flaked, tinned tuna. Mill a little black pepper over the nest and garnish with raw onion rings (or chopped onion) and a pinch of chopped parsley.

YOU WILL NEED:

Dried beans – of almost any kind
Pepper and salt
Vinaigrette
Canned tuna fish (in oil or brine)
Milled black pepper
Onion
Parsley

'You only want me for my body'

31

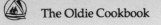

Shrimp Pancakes or Fritters

Make a pancake batter (see p. 166) whisking in a good dash of chilli sauce – Amoy, I think, has the most taste with the least heat.

Buy, say, 8 oz. of cooked peeled shrimps. If you like 'crunch' and believe as I do, that when peeled, shrimps lose most of their taste, head and tail small brown shrimps but do not peel them. Chop up an onion as finely as possible. Add the shrimps and the onion to the batter then allow to rest for an hour or so.

Heat olive oil in a frying pan then put in spoonfuls of the mixture – small dollops for fritters, larger for pancakes. Turn them over when browned on the bottom and continue until cooked right through. Garnish as you will with paprika or parsley.

The fritters are delicious with drinks. The pancakes made a fine hors d'œuvre or light main course.

You will need:
Batter
Chilli sauce
Shrimps
Onion
Olive oil
Parsley or paprika

Decorative Garlic Rice

This is another of those recipes that can be an hors d'œuvre or main course depending upon the quantity served.

Wash the rice (white or brown) thoroughly and extract any dark bits. To ensure the rice is properly washed, agitate it in a metal sieve beneath cold running water. When the water flowing through looks as clear as that issuing from the tap, the rice is ready to cook.

Melt a good lump of butter in a frying pan that has a fitting lid. Add as many crushed cloves of garlic as you desire, then the rice and a good sprinkling of salt. Fry for a minute or two. Now add water – twice the volume of the rice. Cover the pan and simmer the rice until the water has been absorbed and the rice cooked. Check that the rice is not burning towards the end. Add more water if you think it necessary. The cooking time should be about 20 minutes for white rice. Brown rice takes a little longer.

This is an excellent dish served with a main course, but it enters the realms of uniqueness when the hot rice is used as a foil for something cold and preferably colourful, such as any of the following:

Thinly sliced avocado pear; smoked cod's roe; grated carrot; crabmeat; chopped or whole olives; ham slivers; cheese cubes;

smoked salmon; crispy fried boiled Brussels sprouts; salami slices; taramasalata; sardines; crumbled Roquefort; pickled peppers; anchovies; mini beetroots; pickled herring; beansprouts; tuna fish; cucumber; boiled chestnuts; broccoli spears; a thick layer of chopped herb or herbs, or any item that you think will please those for whom you cook.

YOU WILL NEED:
Rice, brown or white
Garlic
Salt
Butter
Any imaginative topping

MODERN HOME COOKING   STEVEN APPLEBY

A Sorrel, Spinach, Chard or Beetroot-leaf Dish

This hors d'œuvre, vegetable or light main course is easy and quick to make and concentrated in taste. It is at its most distinctive when made with sorrel, but other tender green leaves will do.

Strip the green parts of your leaves away from the stemmy bits. Discard the latter. Tear the leaves into smallish pieces.

Heat some oil in a frying pan that possesses a lid. Add a good dash of vinegar, pepper, salt and a tiny pinch of icing sugar. Boil away the vinegar to the stage when you can sniff the steam without choking. Now add the leaves. Cover the pan, and cook the greens slowly until they have turned colour, stirring once in a while (the time will depend on the type of leaves and their quantity).

Remove the lid and stir the cooked greens until any excess moisture has departed. Decant the results into a serving dish. Grate over some cheddar cheese and decorate with a sprinkling of paprika. Serve hot.

If this dish is made in advance, to be served cold on its own, or as a vegetable to accompany another dish, grate over the cheese just before serving, or offer it unadorned.

You will need:

Sorrel, spinach, chard, beetroot tops, or any other edible leaf of a tender nature
Oil
Vinegar
Pepper and salt
Icing sugar
Cheddar cheese (optional)
Paprika (optional)

35

Beans El Salvador

It so happened that a serving lady from El Salvador who was offering these delicious beans at a Costa Rican reception had made them herself. She kindly gave me the recipe, saying that it was one of the most popular dishes in her country.

Soak dried red kidney beans overnight. Drain, then cover well with fresh water and throw in plenty of peeled garlic cloves. Boil rapidly for 15 minutes and for a further hour or so on a low heat. Drain them and conserve their liquid.

Fry the beans in oil with plenty of chopped onion adding, every so often, some of the liquid in which they were boiled. When the onion is cooked add pepper and salt. Stir in some chilli sauce if desired.

Put the beans in a serving dish and offer them hot or cold, sprinkling a little chopped parsley over them at the time of serving.

YOU WILL NEED:

Dried red kidney beans
Garlic
Oil
Onion

Pepper and salt
Chilli sauce (optional)
Chopped parsley

Methi-Leeky

This vegetable dish may be eaten on its own as an hors d'œuvre or with curry. Allow 1 medium leek per person.

Wash the leeks with great thoroughness by peeling off the outer layer and cutting off most of the top leaf and any root. Insert a sharp knife right through the centre and draw it towards the green end, thus dividing the upper part of the leek in half. Open the folds and, holding the leek upside down under running water, rub away any earth that may be lodged there.

Slice the leeks across thinly. Put them in a pressure cooker or saucepan with a little white wine, water, salt, a few cloves, a few cardamoms, a very small piece of cinnamon stick and a good sprinkling of dried methi leaves (fenugreek). Pressure cook for 15–20 minutes or cover and simmer in a saucepan on the stove for around 30 minutes. Finish cooking with the lid off to almost eliminate the liquid content. Arrange in a shallow dish and serve. You can keep this dish warm for a while in a low oven.

YOU WILL NEED:

Leeks
Dry white wine
Salt
Cloves

Cardamoms
Cinnamon stick
Dried methi leaves (fenugreek)

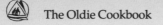

Vegetables with an Eastern Touch

This is a different and delicious way to offer vegetables.

Heat 2 tablespoons of good olive oil and gently fry some finely-chopped fresh ginger and garlic for a minute or two. Now throw in de-seeded green peppers cut into small squares, add pepper and salt and a little vinegar. Cover the pan and cook slowly until the vegetable is soft. If towards the end of cooking there is too much liquid, remove the lid so that the surplus can evaporate.

Put the hors d'œuvre into an attractive dish and allow to cool. Sprinkle with a little extra virgin olive oil. Garnish as you feel fit and serve with warmed bread.

Almost any other vegetable can be cooked in this way: cour-gettes, celery, carrots, Brussels sprouts, mushrooms, aubergines, parsnips, leeks, etc. Of course, some will take longer to cook. Others you may need to boil first – especially if they are of a fibrous, rooty nature.

You may like your vegetables well cooked, or almost raw. Adjust times accordingly.

YOU WILL NEED:

Olive oil
Fresh ginger root
Garlic
Pepper and salt
Vinegar
Green peppers (or almost any other vegetable)
Garnish

Sailors' Mussels

Buy or gather an adequate quantity of similar-sized mussels – say 1 pint or 1 lb. for each person. If gathering them from a rocky shore, select unencrusted ones that have been submerged by each

tide. Let them spit out their sand for an hour or two in a bucket of clean, unsalted water. Then allow them to dry out in a colander.

Prepare mussels for the pot by placing them in a bowl under a running tap. Discard those that float or are heavy (probably full of sand or mud). Give the remainder a good scrub, scraping off any encrustations. Then place them in a bowl and cut off the beards with kitchen scissors, or using strong fingers or pliers, de-beard them by pulling out the filaments with which they once attached themselves to rocks or rope. Place them once more in the colander to drain. They are now ready to cook.

Put a glass or two of dry white wine, a touch of vinegar and a mill or two of black pepper into a large saucepan that allows plenty of space above the shellfish. Bring the wine to the boil. Add the mussels and, with the lid on the pan, give the contents a good shake up and around. Now bring the liquid to a foaming boil.

Take the pan from the heat and shake them again – top to bottom. Once more bring them to the bubbly boil. They should now be steamed open and ready.

Put the opened mussels, with the juices, into a large serving dish or in individual bowls. Sprinkle with chopped parsley and chopped onion. Each person extracts the meat from the opened shells by using a joined shell as a pair of pincers. French bread or, surprisingly perhaps, chips go well with them.

You will need:
Fresh mussels
White wine
Vinegar
Chopped onion
Chopped parsley

Stuffed Mussels

A bag of these stuffed mussels must be one of the most important items for the freezer.

Prepare and cook the mussels as in the previous recipe, then extract them from their shells when cool. (You can use the liquid in which they were cooked for the start of a fish soup, but let all solid matter sink to the bottom before decanting the liquor from above.) While the mussels are drying out, mix plenty of butter, salt, pressed garlic and chopped parsley together. Place each mussel in a half shell and cover and surround with this stuffing, pressing the mixture well down.

Carefully bag up and deep-freeze those that you do not want right away. They may then be extracted in the numbers wanted when an interesting hors d'œuvre or 'instant' meal is called for.

Put the desired number of mussels in an enamelled iron dish or shallow heat-proof container. Then place them under the grill.

When the butter is bubbling well, they are ready to eat. Serve with chunks of hot bread to sop up the juices.

YOU WILL NEED:
Mussels
White wine
Vinegar
Butter
Salt
Pressed garlic
Chopped parsley

Mussels in a Hot Sauce

This is a dish favoured by the Greeks on their north-eastern coast.

After preparing and cooking the mussels as described above, extract them from their shells and put them with their juices in a pan with some pepper and salt, lemon juice, finely-cut green or red chillies (de-seeded) and a little thickening made by mixing a teaspoon or more of cornflour or potato flour with a little cold water.

Cook gently, stirring all the time until the sauce thickens. Serve with lots of hot French bread.

YOU WILL NEED:

Mussels
White wine
Vinegar
Pepper and salt

Lemon juice
Chillies
Cornflour or potato flour

Canaletto's Mussels

My wife decided that a mussel dish served to her in Venice was the best she had ever tasted. I dipped my bread into its juices and agreed. The following is a very rough personal interpretation of that recipe. It is quite delicious. Serve as a first course or light meal.

Clean and de-beard fresh mussels (at least a quart, or 2 lb. for 2 people) as described above, then leave to drain for a while as you will not want excess liquid in the sauce.

Pour plenty of olive oil (say 3 tablespoons if you want to measure it) into a saucepan. Add a good dash of Pernod, ouzo, or similar aniseed spirit, a handful at least of finely-chopped parsley (stems and all can go through a hand-held herb Mouli), a squashed garlic clove or two, the grated skin from a large well-scrubbed lemon, a heaped teaspoon of Dijon mustard, plenty of milled black pepper and a little sea salt. Stir together well, then heat and add the mussels. Cover the pan and toss around over the heat until the mussels are all open.

Lift the mussels on to serving plates using a perforated spoon, and keep them warm. Now boil the sauce so that it reduces to the consistency of thin cream. Pour this over the mussels and serve. An empty double shell can be used as a pincer to extract the flesh from other mussels, and for spooning up the juices. French bread is almost an essential accompaniment.

For those who do not like to mess around with shells at the table, steam open the mussels in a little water, extract them from their shells and put them aside. Heat up the sauce above, add the mussels, heat through and serve. Alternatively, allow them to cool and offer them cold.

You will need:

Mussels	Lemon
Olive oil	Dijon mustard
Pernod, ouzo or similar	Milled black pepper
Fresh parsley	Sea salt
Garlic	

Francis Bacon's Kipper Hors d'œuvre

I had built a house in isolated countryside with a fine studio and one bedroom. When coming to sell it, an estate agent said that no one would want a one-bedroomed house. I advertised it myself and sold the house to Francis Bacon. The simplicity of its soft platforms and unadorned walls of bare plaster appeared as background in many of his paintings.

Inviting me to lunch one day, he had laid out a table in the marble-floored (made of washstand tops) studio that overlooked rolling Berkshire downland. On the white tablecloth, in the form of an Impressionist's still life, were spotless glasses, champagne, white plates, knives and forks, French bread and a dish of this colourful hors d'œuvre. This is how he made it:

Marinate uncooked kipper fillets in a vinaigrette for an hour or so. Then lay them on a plate and cover with the marinade. Decorate with rings of raw onion.

YOU WILL NEED:
Kipper fillets
Vinaigrette
Onion

An Onion Hors d'œuvre

An American friend had rented Bertrand Russell's house in Wales to write a book. I was invited to stay. On arrival, I suggested that I make the evening's hors d'œuvre from whatever I could find in the shops. I was unaware of the wry smiles that greeted this suggestion.

The only food available in a nearby town was lamb, potatoes and onions. I bought onions and in adversity (as is the origin of many an excellent dish), made a surprisingly successful hors d'œuvre. If you are ever caught wanting a first course with only onions at hand, this is an excellent and simple way to deal with them.

Allow at least 1 medium onion per person. Skin and chop them up fairly coarsely then put them into a frying pan with some olive oil. Add pepper and salt and cook the onions slowly until they start to colour, reduce in bulk, and smell of fried onions. Now add a quantity of good wine or cider vinegar (about an eighth of the volume of onions). This will evaporate as you continue with the cooking. Keep stirring.

When you are able to sniff the steam without discomfort, the onions will be pale golden and ready. Pour off any surplus oil and allow the onions to cool. Serve in a pleasing dish and, if you have any, sprinkle with chopped parsley. A supply of good bread is essential for this dish.

YOU WILL NEED:

Onions
Oil
Pepper and salt
Vinegar
Parsley

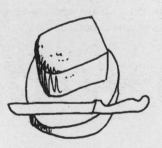

Hock and Red Pepper

Buy a ready-cooked smoked bacon hock, or cook your own (see p. 100).

Skin and bone the hock. Then slice the rosy-coloured meat into thin strips and arrange them in an attractive dish. Test the meat for saltiness then coat with a vinaigrette adjusted for salt content accordingly (see p. 67).

Remove the seeds and stem from a red pepper and finely slice the flesh. Fry gently in a little good oil (preferably olive) until tender, then lay the slices across the meat and pour over the oil from the pan.

This is a lovely combination of colour and tastes.

YOU WILL NEED:

A cooked hock
Vinaigrette
A red pepper
Oil

Sardines and Onions

It was in Venice that a mixed seafood hors d'œuvre contained the following combination which makes an excellent dish on its own.

Fry finely chopped onions in olive oil. As they cook, add pepper, salt and vinegar. When the vinegar has evaporated and the onions are transparent but not yet turning brown, they are ready. Allow them to become cold, then arrange with canned sardines on a shallow serving dish. The addition of a few black olives and a sprinkling of paprika or chopped parsley will transform the appearance.

YOU WILL NEED:

Onions	Canned sardines
Olive oil	Paprika (optional)
Pepper and salt	Parsley (optional)
Vinegar	Black olives (optional)

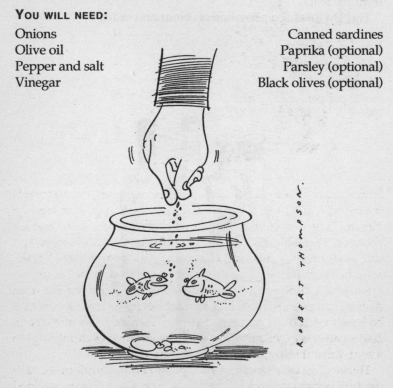

'The food's good but the atmosphere's a little damp'

SOUPS

Soups require more imagination than most dishes. For vegetable soups especially, use a hand-operated Mouli in preference to a blender. For a splendid 'French café' soup, cook your chosen chopped vegetables in butter for a short time. Add pepper and salt, stock or stock cube and water, and simmer until soft. Eat the soup in its chunky state, or put some or all through the Mouli.

Some wonderful soups are made out of the liquid residue from dishes such as boiled beef and carrots, and Irish stew. Others may be based on cooked remains that have included cabbage (see p. 204) – bacon is excellent with these. The addition of dumplings to a soup turns it into a far more substantial dish (see p. 62).

Thickenings may be of egg yolk, potato flour, cornflour, or balls made of butter into which flour has been worked. Potatoes added to vegetable soups will also help to thicken them.

Tomato purée makes a great addition to soups. So too does curry powder – more than a pinch will transform yesterday's soup into today's mulligatawny. Vinegar and sugar enhances soups provided they are not creamy. If used judiciously, good canned soup (such as tomato or consommé) can be a useful addition. Dry sherries go well with soups – especially those that are clear.

Thick cream or soured cream, if added just before serving, will turn a workaday soup into a special one. The final touch of a sprinkling of chopped parsley, dill or fresh coriander over the soup will enhance its looks, and taste. If no herbs are at hand, a pinch of paprika makes a decorative topping.

There is a French country custom called *'faire chabrot'* that is a must if you are not too genteel of nature: when only a spoonful or two of soup remains in your bowl, pour in a little red or white wine, swill it around, and drink it directly from the bowl.

So you see, there are few rules to keep to when making soups. Imagination is the most important ingredient of all.

Leek and Potato Soup

This is one of the most satisfactory of all soups.

Take several leeks. Cut off all but a little of the leafy, green section. Clean thoroughly and rinse out any grit that may lie between the folds. Cut the leeks across into thin slices.

Peel a similar quantity of potatoes (the type can make a great deal of difference, so experiment with varieties) and cut them into small chunks.

Melt an ounce or two of butter in a large saucepan or pressure cooker. Add the leeks and potatoes and stir over a moderate heat for a little while. Well cover with stock, or water and a dissolved stock cube, and add salt and pepper to taste. Pressure cook for 20 minutes, or simmer in a covered saucepan for double that time. Consume with chunks of hot bread.

For a fine variation use sweet potatoes instead of ordinary potatoes. But add a little vinegar before you simmer the soup.

YOU WILL NEED:

Butter	Pepper and salt
Leeks	Stock
Potatoes	

A Chicken Soup

Ships' cooks on coasters are notorious for their consumption of liquor and for weird practices aboard and ashore. One such would, when sober, impress us crew and visiting ladies by preparing a chicken in cream sauce and a chicken soup. The soup was wonderful. This is how it was made:

Having boiled a large chicken (for the dish with cream sauce), he took all bones, skin, giblets and other remains, and boiled them in the original liquor for very much longer with bay leaves, pepper and salt, cloves and onion. He then added some Maggi (I think) flavour-enhancer that found its way into almost all his dishes (as did nutmeg). A stock cube replaces it. He would then strain the liquid into another pot, extract any little pieces of meat – to add to the soup eventually – and throw the residue overboard.

49

To the strained liquid he would add a mugful or so of rice (the end result was about half rice and half liquid) which, barely washed, retained much of its outer starch, and a little turmeric mixed to a paste with water. The soup was then boiled until the rice was very soft, and finally the chicken bits were added.

Much the same soup can be made with the bones and remaining morsels, skin, juices and pan scrapings from a roast chicken.

YOU WILL NEED:

Leftover chicken bones and bits
Bay leaves
Pepper and salt
Cloves

Onion
Stock cube
Rice
Turmeric

A Mushroom Soup

Dried mushrooms are easily obtainable and impart for less cost, more taste to a soup than the fresh variety.

Buy a small handful of dried, sliced mushrooms. Soak in cold water for 24 hours, then strain (conserve the liquid) and, with knife or scissors, cut into small pieces.

Make a white sauce (see p. 64), using milk, stock and the liquor in which the mushrooms were soaked, then add the mushroom pieces. Season and dilute as thought necessary and continue cooking slowly until the mushroom pieces are cooked and the soup amalgamated.

This soup is even better the following day.

YOU WILL NEED:

Dried mushrooms
Butter
Flour
Pepper and salt
Milk
Stock or stock cubes

A Middle-European Kind of Soup

This soup is just the right dish to have ready for those who have been out in the winter cold. The combined smell of cabbage and smoked meat is enough to give anyone a hearty appetite.

Melt an ounce or so of butter in a good-sized pot. Cut up a green cabbage into small pieces and throw these on to the butter. Add a couple of chopped onions and perhaps garlic, and a few potatoes that you have peeled and cut into chunks. Stir together then put in chopped smoked bacon (3–4 rashers) and slices of Polish sausage (boiling ring). Add pepper and salt, then cover with stock.

Simmer on the stove, or in the oven for 30–40 minutes until the vegetables are soft, or pressure cook for half that time.

Don't forget to 'faire chabrot', the French trick described on page 48.

You WILL NEED:

Butter	Smoked bacon
Green cabbage	Polish sausage (boiling ring)
Onion	Stock
Garlic	Pepper and salt
Potatoes	

The Oldie Cookbook

Pumpkin Soup

The pumpkin is a much undervalued vegetable. Usually thought fit only to be hollowed out and candle-lit to keep the ghouls at bay in season, it has many and varied uses in the kitchen. Here is one of them.

Melt an ounce or more of butter in a saucepan and throw in equal quantities of potato and pumpkin and roughly half their volume of chopped onion and grated carrot. Add salt and pepper and cook slowly for 15 minutes, stirring frequently. Then add stock to make up the required quantity and simmer until all the ingredients are tender.

Liquidize or pass the soup through the Mouli. Test for seasoning and stir in single or double cream just before serving.

YOU WILL NEED:

Butter	Carrots
Onions	Pepper and salt
Potatoes	Stock
Pumpkin	Cream

A Sort of Chinese Soup

To good clear stock add a small amount of diced cooked chicken breast and/or lean pork. Stir in a little soy sauce and a dash of sherry or dry white wine. Heat through.

Serve in bowls with strips of lettuce, small pieces of onion top or other fresh edible greenery. What could be simpler!

YOU WILL NEED:

Stock
Diced chicken or pork
Soy sauce
Dry sherry or white wine
Onion tops or other greenery

Jerusalem Artichoke Soup

Many of those who have an internal system that is subject to the generation of air, believe that 'artichoke', especially when turned into soup, should be spelt with an 'F'. However, there is no doubt that Jerusalem artichokes make a wonderful soup.

Melt an ounce or two of butter in a saucepan, throw in a chopped onion and cook gently until soft. Add a pound or two of well scrubbed artichokes (peeled for a whiter, or 'special' soup – see below) and a peeled potato. Season with pepper and salt.

Pour in stock to well cover the contents of the pan and simmer until the vegetables are soft (about 30 minutes). Liquidize, or better still, put through a hand-operated Mouli. Add more stock if necessary to attain the desired consistency. The soup is made.

To turn it into a 'special' dinner-party piece, poach a few scallops in a little milk. Add the milk to the soup. Cut up the scallop meat and add to the soup. Thicken with an egg yolk beaten with some single cream. Heat to the desired temperature, but do not boil. Serve with a sprinkling of paprika.

YOU WILL NEED:	TO MAKE IT SPECIAL:
Butter	A few scallops
Jerusalem artichokes	Milk
A good-sized onion	Egg yolk
A good-sized potato	Single cream
Pepper and salt	Paprika
Stock	

Sorrel Soup

Sorrel probably sends up the first green leaves of the year, so for salads or a fresh green soup it is an invaluable plant for your garden or allotment. The leaves have an appetizing, lemony sharpness to them. Spinach may be used instead but it lacks the unique tang of sorrel.

For the soup, tear off a large bunch of leaves. Wash them and extract any tough, central stem fibres. Melt about 2 oz. of butter in a saucepan. Add the leaves with pepper and salt and cook gently for a while, stirring often. Add stock to make up the amount of soup required and simmer until the leaves are tender.

Purée or hand-Mouli the soup. Add a little milk and the lightest thickening of potato flour or cornflour made into a paste with a little cold water. Heat through and serve with cream swirled into each bowl.

YOU WILL NEED:

Butter
Sorrel leaves (spinach is an alternative)
Pepper and salt
Stock
A little milk
Cornflour or potato flour
Cream

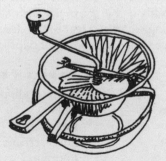

Chicken, Saffron and Swede Soup

This soup is easiest to make if prepared in conjunction with the Chicken on Swede recipe on p. 107. (Withhold some of the mashed, ouzo-flavoured swede or use what is left over.)

Make a good strong chicken stock by boiling up chicken bones, skin, etc., a small onion, a bay leaf and salt and pepper (see also p. 204). Strain the stock into a saucepan and add about 1 lb. of swede, cooked and mashed as on p. 107, and a pinch of saffron dissolved in a little boiling water. Lightly thicken the soup with a small amount of cornflour mixed with cold water.

YOU WILL NEED:

Chicken bones and bits
Stock
Onion
Bayleaf
Pepper and salt
Saffron
Mashed swede
Cornflour

'I've never had much luck with opticians . Have you?'

Five Bean Soup

Here is a hearty soup with which to satisfy a hungry family on a cold winter's day. To make it is simplicity itself, although you'll have to lay plans the day before.

Into a large bowl put smallish quantities of various kinds of dried beans (red kidney, black-eye, broad, haricot, chick peas, black Chinese, or any others at hand) and allow to soak overnight in cold water.

The next day strain them and put them into a large saucepan or pressure cooker with a generous covering of water or stock. Now add a small quantity of dried spaghetti (broken into little pieces), or any other form of pasta, and if desired, some peeled and diced potato. Throw in a peeled garlic clove or two (optional) and add a bay leaf, the contents of a small can of tomato purée, a little sugar, a dash of vinegar, pepper and salt. Now, bring everything up to the boil. If using a saucepan, boil your soup quickly for 10 minutes and then simmer until all the beans are cooked (a further 30–40 minutes). Alternatively, 25 minutes in a pressure cooker will cook them. Extract the bay leaf and adjust the seasoning.

That's it. You have made an excellent, substantial, warming, nourishing (vegetarian), and economical 'filler'.

YOU WILL NEED:

Dried beans	Tomato Purée
Water or stock	Sugar
Dried pasta	Vinegar
Potato (optional)	Bay leaf
Garlic (optional)	Pepper and salt

Fried Onion Soup

First make a good stock of bones, giblets, fresh ginger root, onion, peppercorns, pepper and salt, bay leaf and even a stock cube (see p. 204).

Fry 4–5 chopped up onions in olive oil. When they start to brown and smell like fried onions, add a similar quantity of potatoes, peeled and diced, and a red pepper, de-seeded and cut into small squares. Stir all around. Cook for a little longer, then add the stock and perhaps water. The soup will be ready when the potatoes are soft. A sprinkling of bright green chopped herbs over the top looks good.

YOU WILL NEED:

Stock
Pepper and salt
Onions
Red pepper
Potatoes
Chopped herbs (optional)

Tomato and Pasta Soup

It is always useful to be able to make a quick and simple soup, especially one that children like. The following takes as long to make as pasta does to cook (12 minutes minimum).

In the required volume of stock (or stock cube and water) whisk in the contents of a small can of tomato purée. Now add a handful or two of dried pasta: shells, twists, spaghetti, penne, etc. (or a mixture), a chopped onion, some frozen peas, a dash of vinegar, half a teaspoon of sugar, pepper and salt. Boil until the pasta is soft. Adjust for seasoning, and serve.

It will cook happily for much longer than the normal 12 minutes, and be even better when heated up a second or third time.

You will need:

Stock or stock cubes and water
Tomato purée
Pasta
Onion
Peas
Vinegar
Sugar
Pepper and salt

Potato and Garlic Soup

This is a simple, nourishing soup to make with the retained cooking water from boiling potatoes, cabbage, swede, asparagus, broccoli, etc.

In a saucepan, boil the water with the inclusion of a stock cube and the juice of a lemon. Throw in small chunks of peeled potatoes (say, 2 medium potatoes per pint of water), and at least half a dozen peeled and sliced garlic cloves, previously fried to a golden brown in olive oil. Add pepper and salt.

The soup will be ready when the potato chunks are about to break up. Alter the seasoning if deemed necessary.

YOU WILL NEED:

Water from boiled vegetables
Stock cube
Lemon
Potatoes
Garlic
Olive oil
Pepper
Salt

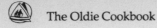

Split Pea Soup

There is a famous soup of this nature in Holland. It is made in many ways, usually elaborate, and served on cold winter days, especially to those on skates. My Dutch wife found this simpler version to be quite acceptable.

Take a couple of handfuls of dried split peas and them soak overnight in a bowl of cold water.

The next day pour all the contents of the bowl into a saucepan or pressure cooker with some stock, or stock cube and water. Season with pepper and salt and add small squares or cubes of smoked bacon. Boil quickly for 10 minutes and then slowly for 30–40 minutes until the split peas are soft and the soup is thickening (25 minutes in the pressure cooker). Add slices of Polish sausage (boiling ring) and cook a little longer. Thicken the soup with a little cornflour dissolved in cold water if you think it necessary.

You will need:
Dried split peas
Stock
Pepper and salt
Bacon
Polish boiling ring sausage
Cornflour

Whatever's Going Soup

This wintery kind of soup is mainly for those who live in the country or have an allotment.

Gather a collection of vegetables – cabbage, chard, beetroot, leaves, parsnips, potatoes, artichokes, swedes, turnips, onions, leeks, carrots – anything going at the time. Wash, peel and remove any woody bits, then cut them up into smallish sections.

Melt an ounce or two of butter in a saucepan or pressure cooker and add the chopped vegetables. Stir them around for a while as they cook in the butter. Add pepper, salt and enough stock to cover well (see p. 204 on making stock). Bring to the boil, cover and simmer for an hour or more, or pressure cook for 20–25 minutes. Serve as it is or puréed if you wish. Soups hardly come simpler or more healthy than this.

YOU WILL NEED:

Butter
Vegetables
Pepper and salt
Stock

'I'll try the Bitter Gourd with Onion Stuffing, followed by Cauliflower with Coconut Milk, Fried Spiced Prawns, Curried Pumpkin and Mango Soufflé'

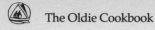
Dumplings for Soup

The addition of dumplings to soups often enhances them and certainly makes them far more substantial. Children love them.

Dumplings are made simply by adding twice the weight or volume of plain or self-raising flour to suet, and with your fingers or a spoon, working them together with a little water to make a firm dough. (Plain flour will make firmer dumplings and take up less space in the pot.) Remember to include salt before adding water. Form the resultant dough into dumplings the size of golf balls. Place them on the surface of the soup 15–20 minutes before the end of the cooking time.

Many flavourings may be added to dumplings, such as fresh or dried herbs, curry powder, grated cheese, chopped onion, garlic, English mustard, caraway seeds, cumin seeds, paprika, turmeric, chopped parsley and others.

YOU WILL NEED:

Flour
Suet
Salt
Optional flavourings

Sauces

A sauce can turn a mundane dish into something special. Not only does it add moisture and richness to fish, meat and vegetables but it can add visual appeal and colour. Most recipe books give a vast number of possible sauces. However, with a few basic recipes and some imagination, a sauce can be created for any occasion. The first and possibly most useful is a white sauce. Vary the liquids and the flavourings to suit whatever you are cooking. Cream soups are often better when started with a white sauce as a basis to which may be added chopped mushrooms, chicken, onions, or other ingredients.

My basic meat sauce is equally versatile, either as a topping for pasta, filling for pancakes, sauce for chilli con carne or as a starting point for numerous other recipes.

There are two other sauces that I find to be invaluable – vinaigrette and mayonnaise. Both are so much nicer when home made, and both may be varied to suit the dish they are to accompany.

The Basic White Sauce

A simple white sauce is the basis for cream soups, herbed sauces, cheese sauce, curry sauce and many others. It is very versatile.

Melt 1½ oz. of butter in a saucepan. Stir in 2 tablespoons of plain flour to make a paste, and plenty of pepper and salt. Whisk it as it heats up, then add around ½ pint of milk, or milk and water, or milk and vegetable water, or fish stock, or stock cube dissolved in water, or whatever liquid was used to cook the object of the dish. The mixture must be stirred vigorously with a whisk all the while, over a high heat at first then low once it has started to thicken. A spoon may be necessary to move the sauce away from the pot angle where the whisk cannot reach. The sauce will thicken as it cooks so dilute as necessary to suit the dish in hand. When it begins to bubble, allow it to cook gently for 5–10 minutes until the taste is no longer floury. Don't stop stirring.

Now add, say, chopped parsley or tarragon for a fish or vegetable sauce; mustard (Dijon or English); capers; grated cheese (be sure to add a dollop of Dijon mustard to the cheese sauce); a little curry powder (stirred into the melted butter) for a French-style curry sauce; or much more curry powder (also worked into the butter) to make a Chinese curry sauce. For the latter, substitute stock in place of milk and add gravy browning for colour. With this sauce you can make an excellent dish simply by adding small slivers of rare (or even raw) lean beef during the last minute of cooking (make the sauce on the thin side).

YOU WILL NEED:
Butter
Plain flour
Pepper and salt
Milk or stock
Flavourings various

Basic Meat Sauce

For anyone with children, or visiting grand-children, and a deep freeze, this must be one of the most important recipes of all. Once made it can be frozen and used as required.

Buy 2 lb. or more of minced beef – not too finely minced. Heat some oil in a large saucepan. Add the beef and stir over a medium heat until it has changed to a brown colour and no lumps remain (best eliminated with a potato masher).

For each 1½ lb. of meat, use a 400 g can (about 14 oz.) of tomato purée. Put the purée into a separate bowl and add water to about 4 times its volume. Whisk together then add a good shake of Worcestershire sauce, a good dash of vinegar and some sugar. Now season with pepper and salt and whisk thoroughly.

Pour this mixture on to the mince and if you like, throw in the contents of a can of chopped tomatoes. Add water to make it fairly liquid then cover and cook very slowly on top of the stove (or in the bottom of an Aga) for around 3 hours, stirring occasionally. Then continue cooking without the lid to reduce the liquid content. Test the sauce for flavour – it might need more salt, sugar or vinegar. Before it has reached true sauce thickness, dissolve a quantity of potato starch or cornflour in cold water and whisk this in. When the mixture has thickened, take the pan off the heat and allow to cool.

Use this sauce for lasagne, spaghetti and other pasta. For chilli con carne add mild chilli-con-carne powder to the sauce then stir it into soaked and well-boiled red beans – adding oil before it is served. To make keema and peas add curry powder and fresh or frozen peas (equal volume of peas to sauce), and stir over the heat until the peas are cooked.

You will need:

Minced beef
Tomato purée
Chopped tomatoes (optional)
Worcestershire sauce
Pepper and salt
Vinegar
Sugar
Cornflour or potato flour

Vinaigrette

The basic vinaigrette is made of 1 part vinegar to 3 or 4 parts oil, or even less vinegar to oil. It all depends on your taste and your vinegar. Home-made wine vinegar made with a 'mother', for instance (see p. 201) can be very strong. Vinegars may be flavoured (by the manufacturer or you) with herbs, spices or even fruit such as raspberries.

Then there is the choice of oil to be made – soy bean, olive, sunflower, walnut, hazelnut, safflower – some even add cream. So the basics can vary enormously in quantity and taste. That is the delight of vinaigrette.

Having mixed your oil and vinegar, add salt and pepper to taste, I usually add powdered English mustard and sugar (icing-sugar is the easiest to use). To ensure against the formation of little lumps, these dry ingredients must be placed on the liquid line in the bowl and rubbed into the vinegar/oil mixture with the back of a wooden spoon. You can bottle your vinaigrette to shake up and use when wanted.

Further possible additions include herbs, both fresh and dried, capers, brined green peppercorns, garlic, sesame seeds (or any other aromatic seeds) chopped olives and diced onion or shallot. All are grist to your mill. Let your imagination run riot.

However, the basic oil/vinegar/pepper/salt mixture is often the best vinaigrette for green salads, and remember that it shouldn't be added until the very last minute.

You will need:
Vinegar
Oil
Salt and pepper
Mustard (optional)
Sugar (optional)

Mayonnaise

Mayonnaise is not only quick and easy to concoct but, for some reason, your ability to make it will impress those at your table.

Use mayonnaise as a sauce for many an hors d'œuvre, salad, or cold main course. Once it has been made, add herbs, garlic or any other flavours you choose.

A heavy bowl or mortar is the best vessel in which to make mayonnaise, but any bowl will do. For ease, make it in the serving dish.

Be sure that the eggs are very fresh and that their source is hygienic and healthy. Otherwise, base your mayonnaise on a manufactured variety (see below).

One egg yolk will make quite a volume. Separate the yolk from the white of egg and put it into the bowl. Now add almost the same volume of Dijon mustard (Amora is one of the best) and stir them together. A touch of lemon juice added at this point will give some 'bite' to the mayonnaise, but it is not essential.

Now slowly dribble in vegetable oil or olive oil (or both) stirring continually. The yolk and mustard will absorb a lot of this oil and the mayonnaise will become thicker as you proceed. Just a drop or two of added water will alter its consistency for the better, but again, this is not crucial. That's it.

Tackling the job with aplomb will ensure success every time. But try to keep the ingredients at roughly the same temperature. This method is fail-safe. An alternative way is as follows:

Mix together equal parts of bought mayonnaise, egg yolk and Dijon mustard, then slowly add oil to obtain the right consistency.

For those fearful of salmonella, work some Dijon mustard and olive oil into bought mayonnaise. Enliven it with pressed garlic or chopped herbs, or turn it into a sauce tartare by adding a mixture of chopped onion or shallot, cut-up olives, capers and gherkins.

YOU WILL NEED:

Egg yolk
Dijon mustard
Lemon juice (optional)

Oil
Salt and pepper

A Sharp Sauce

This is a lovely sauce to pour over slices of hot or cold cooked meat – especially boiled tongue and ham.

Heat a tablespoon of two of oil, butter or dripping in a pan. Add about ½ oz. of flour, a dash of both gravy browning and Dijon mustard, pepper and salt. Stir around and cook through gently.

Now slowly add around ¼ pt. of vinegar, stirring as you go. Allow the acids to evaporate until you reach the stage of being able to place your nose into the rising vapours without discomfort. Add plenty of capers and chopped gherkins before pouring it over the meat.

YOU WILL NEED:

Oil, butter or dripping
Flour
Gravy browning
Dijon mustard
Pepper and salt
Vinegar
Capers and gherkins

Natural Juices and other Gravies

Fry pieces of veal, beef, chicken, lean chops or steak in butter and oil, or dripping, or other oil or fat. When done, lift out the meat, and pour any fat into the dripping-pot. Add half a glassful of dry white wine to the pan. Stir around over the heat until the cooked morsels that have stuck to the hot surface become loose and dissolve. Strain these juices if you must, and quickly pour the simply contrived and sumptuous liquid over the pieces of meat. You will have made an exquisite 'gravy'.

Now for more traditional gravy to accompany a joint.

If you keep a pot of dripping in your refrigerator, your first move must be to cut around the hard dripping cap, lifting it out to reveal a layer of delicious jelly. Tip this out and keep it ready for your gravy. When the joint is cooked, set it on one side and pour off most of the fat from the roasting pan into the dripping pot. Put your pan on the heat and allow the residual liquids to bubble gently.

Add a sprinkling of flour (not too much), pepper and salt and a dash of gravy browning (for appetizing colour). Stir it all around allowing the flour to cook. Now add the jelly that you have previously extracted from the dripping pot, along with water, stock, stock cube dissolved in water, liquid from any vegetables that you may have boiled, wine, tea, or whatever you fancy in order to reach the desired consistency for your gravy.

A dash of vinegar and a pinch of sugar will always improve a gravy (as they will a stew). A shake of tomato ketchup will give it zest and flavour, so will a dash of Worcestershire sauce. Taste for seasoning and adjust if thought necessary. Strain the gravy if you feel that way inclined, and serve as you will.

Any gravy left over after the meal can start, or be added to a soup. And note that if you have been adding various pan fats to your dripping mixture, once in a while put the pot into the oven to amalgamate its contents. The jellies will then sink to form one layer at the bottom, in readiness for your next gravy.

YOU WILL NEED:

Natural pan juices
Flour
Gravy browning
Pepper and salt
Jelly from the dripping pot
Stock liquid of your choice
Vinegar and sugar
Tomato ketchup and/or Worcestershire sauce (optional)

Bread Sauce

We seem to eat bread sauce only with turkey at Christmas time, but it goes splendidly with all sorts of meat at any other time. It is an undervalued sauce, and under used. My Dutch relations were introduced to it one Christmas. They had not heard of it before, and had no idea how it had been made. They loved it.

We may all have different ideas on how to make bread sauce. Here is my recipe.

Gently boil ½ pt. or more of milk to which you have added plenty of finely-chopped onion and a small onion stuck with half a dozen or more cloves. When thoroughly cooked, discard the cloved onion and add a large lump of butter and plenty of pepper and salt. Allow the butter to melt, then stir in 1–2 handfuls of finely rubbed breadcrumbs, gained from the middle of a white loaf that is at least a day old. Test for seasoning. Keep the sauce on the thin side as it will thicken of its own accord in the serving dish.

Serve hot with almost any meat.

YOU WILL NEED:

Milk
Onions
Cloves
Butter
Pepper and salt
White breadcrumbs

Vegetables and Salads

These recipes are equally good served on their own in the French manner as they are when accompanying a meat or fish dish. If you favour a vegetarian diet, alter the volumes to suit your own requirements.

Try not to combine delicately flavoured vegetables with strong flavoured foods. Their tastes are easily masked.

Let vegetables speak for themselves. The main point to remember is not to overcook them. Most have wonderful tastes to reveal if handled with care.

Aubergine as Vegetable

This is one of the best ways to cook aubergine as a vegetable to accompany another dish. It may also be eaten on its own.

Fill a kitchen basin with water and dissolve in it a tablespoon of salt.

Cut the aubergine in ¼-inch slices and put them into the water. They will float. Leave for an hour, turning over once in a while.

Extract and dry them, dip them in plain flour and fry in olive oil until brown on both sides and soft in the middle.

YOU WILL NEED:
Aubergine
Salt
Plain flour
Olive oil

Potato Pancakes

One of the quickest and easiest ways of turning the humble potato into something special is simply to grate it (raw) in little piles straight into hot oil in a frying pan. Form the piles into thin, separate flat pancakes. Sprinkle a little pepper and salt over them and fry until both sides are golden brown. There is no need to waste time in peeling the potato. Different varieties respond to this treatment in different ways.

Alternatively, the potato may be peeled, grated into a bowl, then salted and drained of excess moisture before mixing with a beaten egg and grated onion. Fry as before.

Another variation is to grate cheese into a bowl before adding a beaten egg and the grated, drained potato. A little grated nutmeg will further enhance the flavour.

These small potato pancakes go well with anything from fried or scrambled egg, to steak, cutlets, roast chicken, game or the Sunday joint. Quick to prepare and cook, they are ideal fare when arriving home late and hungry.

YOU WILL NEED:

Potato
Oil
Pepper and salt
Egg, chopped onion, cheese and nutmeg are all optional extras

Acorn Squash Twice Over

A favourite vegetable in America, acorn squash (Table Ace in UK seed shops), is now often seen in UK supermarkets. Because of its rock-hard skin, it stores happily throughout the winter.

Halve an acorn squash from top to bottom (a saw may be necessary) and extract the pips from the cavity. Oil the surface of both its yellow flesh and green skin. Sprinkle the exposed surface with pepper and salt and bake the halves, cavity uppermost, for an hour or more in a medium oven until soft.

Serve hot in its skin, which is now very edible. It is especially good when offered with cold meat or a 'musseau' (see p. 144).

If you bake more than you need you could use those left over as follows:

Thoroughly heat the remaining halves under the grill, break an egg into each cavity and coat with grated Cheddar cheese. Return them to the grill until the eggs are cooked to your satisfaction.

There are other members of the squash family that will succumb to this treatment happily.

YOU WILL NEED:

Acorn squash – or other variety
Oil
Pepper and salt

FOR THOSE LEFT OVER:

Eggs
Cheddar cheese

Mashed Potato

Mashed potato is a most wonderful buffer to rich food, and an excellent sopper-up of delicious juices.

The basic method is as follows:

Boil potatoes in lightly salted water until they give way to the point of a sharp knife. Drain off all the water (using it for soup, stock or sauces if you can) and when dry, mash out all the lumps. Then add a large piece of butter and plenty of pepper and salt. Stir in enough milk to obtain the consistency required then mash and beat to a smooth mixture. For pie toppings use less butter and keep the mix on the dry side.

Variations on the theme: use extra virgin olive oil instead of butter; beat in pressed garlic; consider capers or cut-up stoned olives; mix in green peppercorns, slices of cornichons and morsels of cooked red peppers; add a chopped herb, dried or fresh; add lemon juice to give it sharpness.

Formulate a combination of several of these ingredients in your experimentations, and you will have made a splendid mash – a dish in its own right.

If you make a sloppy mash by adding more than the usual amount of butter and milk (it will absorb a great deal of liquid), place it in the oven in a fireproof dish and it will rise and brown in a most delightful way.

Sprinkle toasted breadcrumbs over the surface of a mashed-potato pie topping to give it a crunchy topping.

If you have some plain mashed potato left over from a meal, it can be used as a topping for all sorts of pies such as fish (see p. 137), chicken and leek, game, vegetable, as well as for cottage or shepherd's pie.

You can fry it plain to be enjoyed with eggs or sausages. Alternatively, mix it with tinned tuna or smoked fish, adding chopped parsley to form fishcakes; or mix it with corned beef and fried onion to make corned-beef hash. In both cases fry the mixture, turning it over at the half way stage when the under side is crisp.

Another delicious way of using up leftover mash is to put it into

The Oldie Cookbook

a bowl with flour and a beaten egg. Work the mixture together with milk to make a 'dough' then roll it out to form a top for such as steak and kidney or fruit pies.

Fry small discs or cubes of mash to serve hot with cold salads.

Work in grated cheese and Dijon mustard. Roll and cut into strips to be baked in the oven as finger food when serving drinks.

And on it goes. Mash is very versatile.

YOU WILL NEED:

Potatoes
Butter
Pepper and salt
Milk
Imagination

Brussels Sprouts

Firm, dark, tight little sprouts are best. Trim them, boil for no more than 5 minutes, drain, return to the hot empty pan to dry, and serve directly – preferably as a dish on its own with a little butter, pepper and salt.

For another excellent dish, cook the sprouts as above then leave (until the next day if you like) in a bowl. When dry, fry them in oil and butter until they begin to crisp on the outside and take on a glorious smell. Incorporate a crushed clove of garlic as you are frying them. You can of course simply use leftover sprouts for this dish. It would be worth ensuring there were enough by cooking far too many for your initial requirements!

Produced either way, these simple dishes are excellent.

YOU WILL NEED:

Brussels sprouts
Butter
Oil
Pepper and salt
Garlic

Bacon in Brussels

Boil trimmed Brussels sprouts for 5 minutes. As you are doing this, fry some small pieces of rindless, thinly sliced, smoked streaky bacon until they are crisp. Pour off any excess fat. Then in your serving dish make a vinaigrette using olive oil (see p. 67).

Drain the sprouts and dry them off by shaking them in the pan over the heat for a little while. Then toss them in the vinaigrette, add the crisp bacon bits and serve.

YOU WILL NEED:

Brussels sprouts
Bacon (rindless, smoked streaky)
Vinaigrette

A Classic Way to Cook Tomatoes

This classic dish also makes a fine hors d'œuvre. Cook it in the fireproof dish in which it is to be served – it will look and smell so good at the table.

Cut large, meaty tomatoes in half. Place these halves, cut side up, in a fireproof serving dish. Scoop out a little of the pulp from each, putting this in the base of the dish. Press some chopped garlic into each cavity and fill up with olive oil, some of which will spill over to good effect. Add plenty of pepper and salt, then sprinkle over a chopped herb of some sort – sage, parsley, chives, marjoram, sweet basil, coriander, dill – all are delicious. Cover with a layer of toasted breadcrumbs.

Place the dish under the grill and cook until each tomato structure is disintegrating. In other words, cook well. Apportion them with their juices at the table and serve with plenty of bread with which to sop up the succulent liquid.

These tomatoes may also be cooked in a hot oven. This is the better method if they are small or over-ripe and mushy.

YOU WILL NEED:

Tomatoes
Garlic
Olive oil
Pepper and salt
A herb
Toasted breadcrumbs

Salsify

Salsify, that thin, parsnip-like root vegetable, has a delicate taste all its own. It should be presented at the table simply dressed with butter or a sauce that will not drown its flavours.

Peel the salsify and cut it into even-sized lengths. It will become brown and unsightly when the inner flesh is exposed to air, so drop the sections quickly into a water and vinegar mixture until wanted.

Boil the roots until tender (about 25 minutes). Drain them, reserving their cooking liquid, then place them in a serving dish to keep warm. Make a white sauce (see p. 64) using some of the cooking liquid as well as milk. Stir in a handful of very finely chopped parsley. Coat the salsify with this sauce and serve.

Should you grow this vegetable in your garden or allotment, allow a plant or two to flower and seed. The brilliant blue or yellow flowers will open only throughout the morning, closing in the afternoon. The seed heads take the form of large, brown, powder-puffs. Just one of these will provide you with many more seeds than you require for the following year.

YOU WILL NEED:
Salsify roots
Vinegar
White sauce
Parsley

Cauliflower and Crumbs

I came across this excellent way to cook cauliflower in a small restaurant in the Loire on one of my earliest trips to France. It was the first dish to be cooked on my return to England and I have enjoyed it countless times since.

Steam/boil a cauliflower in a little water in a covered saucepan. Do not overcook. Once cooked, allow to dry thoroughly, then break off florets and fry them in butter and oil with some crushed garlic. At the same time fry some breadcrumbs in butter and oil until they are crispy brown. Keep turning them round as they cook or they will suddenly catch and burn. They will need pepper and plenty of salt.

Put the fried florets and cooking juices on a serving dish and cover with the crumbs. They come very hot from the pan so be careful not to burn your mouth.

YOU WILL NEED:
Cauliflower
Butter and oil
Garlic
Breadcrumbs
Pepper and salt

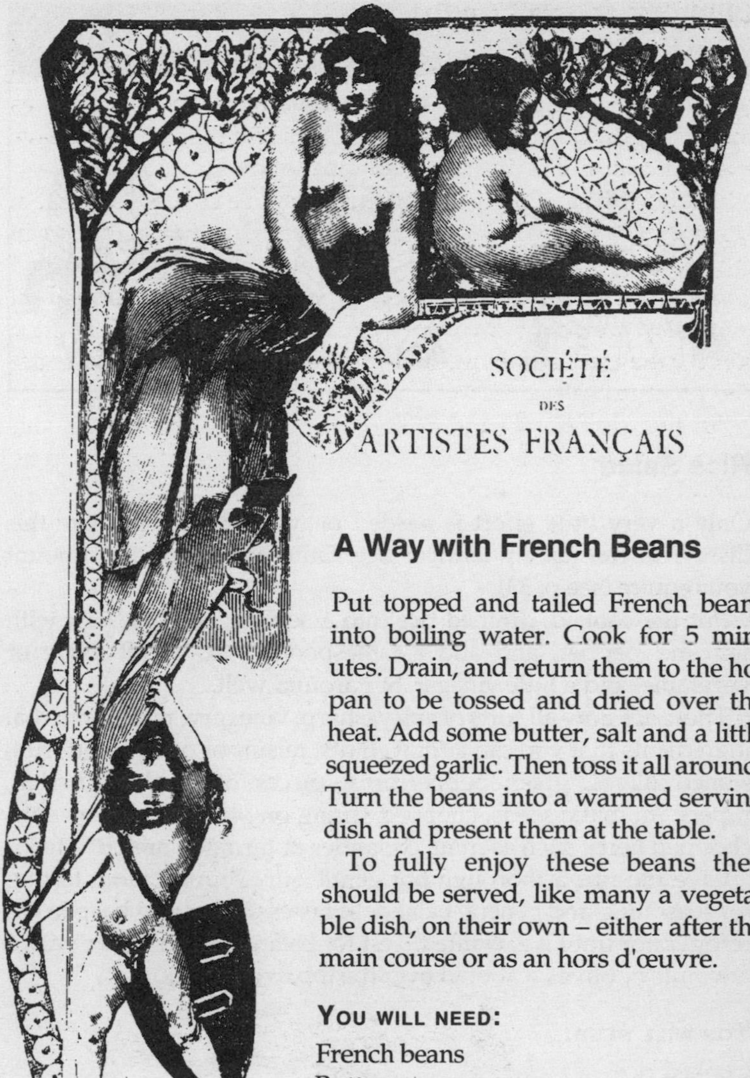

SOCIÉTÉ

DES

ARTISTES FRANÇAIS

A Way with French Beans

Put topped and tailed French beans into boiling water. Cook for 5 minutes. Drain, and return them to the hot pan to be tossed and dried over the heat. Add some butter, salt and a little squeezed garlic. Then toss it all around. Turn the beans into a warmed serving dish and present them at the table.

To fully enjoy these beans they should be served, like many a vegetable dish, on their own – either after the main course or as an hors d'œuvre.

YOU WILL NEED:

French beans
Butter
Salt
Garlic

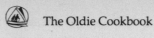

Rice Salad

Only a very little effort is needed on your part to prepare this dish. You can use up leftover rice. Otherwise, cook the amount you require (see p. 33).

Put the cooked, drained rice into a serving bowl, season with salt and pepper, and add a tablespoon or so of oil (olive or vegetable) and a little vinegar. Stir around well.

There are now all sorts of spicy, sharp, vinegary, nutty or herbal ingredients that you can add: walnuts, raisins or other dried fruit, stoned olives, green peppercorns, pieces of pickled gherkin, capers, aromatic seeds, chopped spring onion tops, beansprouts, chopped herbs such as mint, coriander or tarragon are but a few.

Give the rice a thorough but gentle stir-around before testing for seasoning and general balance of tastes. Cover and keep in the refrigerator until it is wanted. Test for balance again. Serve with a few nuts or olives scattered over the top as decoration.

YOU WILL NEED:
Cooked rice
Oil and vinegar
Salt and pepper
An assortment of flavouring ingredients

Roast Vegetables

This is an excellent way of cooking soft-textured vegetables when you are roasting meat. The best vegetables to use are peppers, chicory (endive), aubergines (eggplant), onions, leeks, courgettes and celery. Divide the peppers and aubergines into quarters lengthwise, chicory in halves lengthwise, courgettes and leeks in slices, onions in rings and celery in sticks.

Put the vegetables in a roasting pan, dribble over olive oil and season with salt and pepper. About ¾ hour before the meat will be done put the pan in the oven. Baste with the oil in the pan at least once while they are cooking, and occasionally check how they are doing.

Any roast vegetables left over may be used as an hors d'œuvre for another meal.

You will need:

Soft vegetables
Olive oil
Pepper and salt

Fennel and Chicory Salad

Make a strong vinaigrette (see p. 67). Chop raw fennel root and chicory into pieces of an edible size then toss them in the vinaigrette. Serve immediately.

Small squares of red pepper may be added for colour and extra taste.

YOU WILL NEED:

Fennel root
Chicory (endive)
Vinaigrette
Red pepper (optional)

Potatoes in Batter

This is a rather delicate way of serving potatoes. And they look wonderful too.

Have ready some Yorkshire pudding batter (see p. 184) made with self-raising flour. Peel potatoes, cut them into small chunks and fry until soft in plenty of olive oil. Season with pepper and salt. Pour the Yorkshire pudding mixture over the potatoes to almost half their depth.

Fry slowly (with the lid on) until the batter is almost cooked through (15–30 minutes). Remove the lid and turn the mixture over to brown the other side. When done, slide it on to a serving dish, and if liked, sprinkle over some chopped parsley.

Eat as a vegetable on its own, or with hot or cold meat.

YOU WILL NEED:

Potatoes   Yorkshire pudding batter
Olive oil   Chopped parsley (optional)
Pepper and salt

Carrots and Potatoes – Deliciously Different

New carrots are delicious just lightly boiled and tossed in butter, with crushed garlic, chopped parsley and a trace of salt added.

For a vegetarian main dish, serve the carrots with mashed potato made in the following way:

Boil the potatoes, then mash them well adding plenty of butter, pepper and salt. Now add enough milk to make a sloppy consistency. Put the mixture into a heat-proof dish and bake in a moderate oven until the potato rises and browns.

The combination of colours and tastes is magnificent.

YOU WILL NEED:

New carrots
Butter
Garlic
Parsley
Pepper and salt
Potatoes
Milk

Carrot Salad

Grate carrots. Stir in a light oil, such as soy bean, (although olive oil will do) and lemon juice. Serve quickly.

Could anything be simpler, more delicious or healthier?

YOU WILL NEED:

Carrots
Oil
Lemon juice

St. Peter's Cabbage

One of the great advantages of this delicious and 'creamy' vegetable dish is that it can be cooked on the barbecue with the joint. It may also be cooked in the oven.

Halve a cabbage from stem to crown. Drumhead cabbages are best, with their outer leaves green, interior white and tight leaf configuration. Other cabbages will do.

Place a half cabbage, cut side uppermost, on a sheet of foil. Dribble 1–2 tablespoons of good olive oil into the tight gaps between the internal leaves. Now spread at least 2 crushed cloves of garlic over the oiled surface. Sprinkle with salt (sea salt for preference), and mill plenty of black pepper on top of the salt. Make an airtight parcel of the cabbage and cook it on the barbecue or place it in the oven with the joint for as long as you cook the meat.

Lift the cabbage from the hot foil and serve with the juices in which it was cooked.

You will need:

Drumhead cabbage (or other)
Olive oil
Garlic
Salt
Milled pepper

Main Courses

Now we come to what many people regard as the most important part of the meal and that to which they give the most time and thought. You will find that nearly all my ideas are simple in conception and preparation – throw in this and that, clamp on the lid, roughly time, and eat. That is the spirit and style of most of the recipes in this book. My pressure cooker is a great help. It cuts the cooking time drastically and mingles the flavours to give really tasty results. If you have a microwave oven you will be able to adapt a lot of the recipes. Many of these dishes are complete meals in themselves, needing only crusty French bread to mop up the juices. Elsewhere, I have suggested a vegetable, but use what is available in the garden or allotment.

Peppered Shin

Here is a dish that is typical of those I favour, in that it is quick and simple to make, cheap, and gives off delicious smells as it cooks. This masterpiece of simplicity is based very loosely on cathedral workers' fare in medieval Italy, where the cooking was done in earthenware containers in a kiln with the bricks.

Take an iron pot with a lid. In the bottom, place a large number of peeled garlic cloves (at least a head). Lay on top 2-inch chunks of shin of beef (cut from the fore-quarter is best) and sprinkle over salt.

Now open a can of chopped tomatoes (allow a 14 oz., 400 g can per 2 lb. of beef) and pour the contents over the meat. Make sure that the meat is almost covered by liquid. You may need to add water.

Now take your pepper mill of black peppercorns, set it to the coarsest degree by slackening off the nut at the top, and go on grinding the pepper over the surface of meat and liquid until you wrist feels weak – well, add an awful lot, anyway. The dish will take it.

Cover the pot and place in a low oven, or on the lowest heat on top of the stove, for about 3 hours. Then remove the lid and give it another hour – or enough time to reduce the liquid to the state of a thick sauce. Keep an eye on things as they are cooking, to see that nothing sticks to the bottom of the pot. Even give it a gentle prod and a shake to confirm that all is well. You may need to add water.

Put the pot on the table and serve the meat with chunks of hot bread (torn from the loaf) to sop up the spicy juices. Rice or mashed potato are alternatives.

YOU WILL NEED:

Garlic
Shin of beef
Salt
Canned tomatoes
Milled black pepper

Shin 'n' Mushrooms

This dish may be made quickly in the pressure cooker or cooked much more slowly in the oven, accompanied by baked potatoes.

Cut some shin of beef (1 lb. or so) into pieces of an edible size, or ask the butcher to do this for you.

Melt about 1 oz. of dripping, butter or oil of your choice in a pressure cooker or iron pot. Throw in a finely-chopped onion and once it has heated through add pepper and salt, then the beef. Stir around, then put in a pig's trotter, cleaned and split. Add plenty of (preferably wild) mushrooms, sliced if they are large, but otherwise left whole. Pour in a little water or stock – no more than half a pint – and cover the pot.

Cook in a lowish oven for 2 hours, or pressure cook for a little over half an hour. Extract the trotter (throw it away or eat it separately with a vinaigrette, see p. 67).

The feast is ready. Serve with rice, mashed potatoes or, if you are oven-cooking the dish, baked potatoes.

YOU WILL NEED:

Shin of beef
Onion
Cooking oil or fat
Pig's trotter
Mushrooms
Pepper and salt
Water or stock

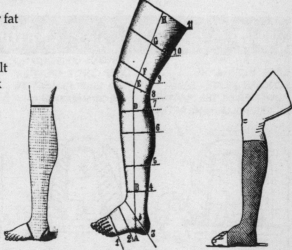

Boiled Beef

Pickled meat is often difficult to find in the shops. But the salting operation can be done quite easily at home. The result is a rare treat.

At least 2 days before you want to eat it, buy some rolled and tied brisket or other cut, weighing 3 lb.

Put a gallon of water into a plastic bucket, add two good handfuls of common salt and a pinch of saltpetre (from the chemist) and allow to dissolve. Add the beef. The following day turn the meat around. When 2 days are up, take it out and keep in the refrigerator until wanted (it will keep for several days).

Soak the beef in water for a few hours before you are ready to put it into the pot, changing the water from time to time.

Heat some water in a pot that will fit the meat, a large quantity of carrots and several dumplings. Add the beef, a small peeled onion or two, and a dozen or so black peppercorns. Bring to the boil, cover and simmer for 2 hours. After 1 hour, add the carrots, sliced, and half an hour later the dumplings (see p. 62).

Make some fresh English mustard as an accompaniment, and serve the beef on a large plate, surrounded by the carrots, dumplings and juices.

If you think that more dumplings will be needed than can fit in with the beef, retain some liquid in the pot and put in more dumplings to cook at the time of serving. They will be ready in 20 minutes. Any liquid and vegetables left over will make a wonderful soup for the next day.

YOU WILL NEED:
Pickled beef or beef to pickle
Onions
Black peppercorns
Carrots
Dumplings
Freshly-made English mustard

Ox-tail

This recipe relies for its success on simplicity and long, slow cooking. Buy lean ox-tail. There is no point in wasting money on fat that will be discarded later.

Soak the pieces in salted water for as long as you like. Dry them and roll in seasoned flour. Heat butter and oil in an iron pot or pressure cooker. Brown the pieces all over then lift them out on to a plate.

In the residual butter and oil fry plenty of chopped onion until brown and smelling of fried onion. Return the pieces of ox-tail to the pot. Stir in a little of the leftover seasoned flour, a little more pepper and salt if thought necessary, enough stock to cover, gravy browning and a dash of vinegar. Cover the pot and cook in a low oven for 3 hours at least. It can also be cooked in the pressure cooker for 35 minutes or more. But it will be better if then transferred to a fireproof pot and given time in the oven.

If you have bought fatty ox-tail, allow the stew to become cold, then spoon off any surface fat before re-heating the meat in its juices.

A sprinkling of chopped parsley makes a good garnish when serving this dish at the table.

Ox-tail is ideal for parties as exact timing is unnecessary, and with the oven on, it makes sense to use this heat to bake potatoes in their skins.

YOU WILL NEED:
Lean ox-tail
Flour
Pepper and salt
Butter
Oil
Onion
Stock
Gravy browning
Vinegar
Chopped parsley

A Party Leg in Wine

Here is a splendid and robust winter party dish that is easy to make but takes time.

Tie up a 2–3 lb. piece of leg or shin of beef several days before you want to eat it. Leave it in the refrigerator covered in a marinade of red wine, a little gravy browning, a dash of olive oil, some sliced onions, a herb or two (or *bouquet garni*), a bay leaf, half a lemon, salt and pepper. Occasionally turn it over in its marinade.

On the day of your meal, extract the meat, dry it and roll in seasoned flour. Melt 2–3 tablespoons of olive oil or good dripping in a large iron pot. Brown the beef in this, then stir in the rest of the seasoned flour (a dessertspoon or so). Cook for a while then pour the marinade over the meat and add 2 pig's trotters.

Cover the pot well and cook the meat for 4–6 hours in a low oven, occasionally checking the moisture content.

Extract the trotters. (You could eat them later dressed in a vinaigrette, p. 67), the lemon and *bouquet garni*. Put the meat on a serving dish and cover with its rich gravy. Cut generous slices and serve with mashed potato.

If there is any beef left over, slice when cold, put it into a deep, tight-fitting dish. Warm any remaining juices and pour them over the meat. Refrigerate, and eat the cold meat in its jelly.

YOU WILL NEED:

Leg or shin of beef in one piece
Red wine
Gravy browning
Olive oil or dripping
Onions
Herbs or *bouquet garni*
Bay leaf
Lemon
Flour
Pig's trotters
Pepper and salt

Tipsy Pig

One of the great advantages of this simple recipe is that the pork chops gain a lovely colour and do not dry out when cooked. A son once complained at table that what he didn't like about Tipsy Pig was that he couldn't tell the difference between the lean (liked) and the fat (disliked), so much alike are they when cooked. However, trim off the excess fat anyway.

Take a shallow dish, the size depending on the number of chops (or other lean pieces of pork) required. Lay the chops on the bottom. Slice lots of peeled garlic cloves and place them around and over the chops. Add salt, pepper, and a herb, such as thyme. Now almost cover the meat with red wine.

Do this in the morning for an evening meal, but turn the chops over a few times during the day. If you cannot manage this, completely cover the chops with wine when you are preparing the dish. But this will provide you with a little more liquid than is necessary.

When you are ready to cook, pour off the wine and keep it aside. Dry the chops. Heat some olive oil in a frying pan and fry the chops slowly with the garlic. When cooked lift out the meat and arrange on a warmed serving dish.

Pour the wine marinade into the frying pan with all the fried residues, brown garlic pieces and herb. Cook for a short time until it bubbles and reduces a little, while stirring it all around and scraping off the bits that will have become attached to the frying pan. You will now have formed a brown and very tasty sauce with which to cover the chops.

Serve with mashed potato, rice or a plain, boiled or steamed vegetable.

YOU WILL NEED:

Pork chops (or lean pork pieces)
Red wine
Garlic

Thyme or another herb
Pepper and salt
Olive oil

Pickled Pork and Asparagus Sauce

Take a hunk of pork (leg if you have got money, a lesser cut if not much, hock if almost none) and leave it in salted water for as long as you like.

Snap the tender parts off asparagus sticks and put them in the bottom of a pressure cooker or pot. Add some pepper but no salt. Pour in a quarter of a bottle of dry Montilla. Add the pork.

Cook in the pressure cooker for 25 minutes or in a covered saucepan for about an hour (or longer for lesser cuts). If using the latter, you will have to check on the liquid content every so often.

Take out the pork once it is cooked and keep it warm on a dish. Reduce the juices a bit if you think it is necessary, then thicken with a little cornflour mixed with cold water. Cook for a little longer. Then put juice and asparagus through a Mouli, or if abso-

lutely no woody bits of asparagus have been included, an electric blender. (Note that if fresh asparagus is not available, add canned pieces to the juices once you have taken out the pork, and allow to heat through.)

Slice the pork and serve it with the sauce. (You can keep it warm in the oven sliced in its sauce, if desired). Salad and new potatoes are good accompaniments.

YOU WILL NEED:

Pork
Pepper
Asparagus
Dry Montilla
Pepper
Cornflour

Leftover Pork and Sharp Apple Sauce

Recipes for leftover meats are always useful. For this, make sure that there is both roast pork and apple sauce left over.

Mince the cooked pork, put it in a bowl and add a little flour, pepper, salt, a beaten egg and plenty of chopped sage. Stir well, adding more flour if necessary to form the mixture into rissoles.

Chop up and fry 2–3 onions in oil or dripping. When the onion is nearly cooked, add a large dash of vinegar. Continue cooking until this evaporates, then stir in the apple sauce. You may need more liquid. Add the rissoles and cook them slowly in the sauce. Serve with acorn squash (p. 76), Brussels sprouts or a green salad.

YOU WILL NEED:

Leftover pork	Onions
Flour	Oil or dripping
Pepper and salt	Vinegar
Egg	Apple sauce
Sage	

Pork and Steamed Vegetables

Soak any cheap cut of pork in a light brine (a tablespoon of salt dissolved in 2 pints of water) for a day.

Rinse the pork and put it into an iron cooking vessel or any other lidded pot. Fill the pot with cider to just cover the meat. Add some black peppercorns, a few cardamoms, a pinch or two of cumin or caraway seeds and a clove or two of garlic (there should be enough salt from the pork). Surround with small whole or cut-up large carrots and cover with thickly-sliced raw potato. With the lid firmly in place, cook gently on top of the stove for 2 or more hours.

Carve the meat and serve it with the vegetables and liquor.

YOU WILL NEED:

A cheap cut of pork	Cider
Peppercorns	Garlic
Cardamoms	Carrots
Cumin or	Potatoes
Caraway seeds	

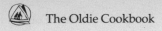

Hock and Split Peas

This simple, cheap and nutritious dish is enjoyed by adults and children alike.

Take a smoked, uncooked bacon hock (usually 1–2 lb.) and soak it in plenty of cold water overnight. Soak a quantity of yellow split peas for the same length of time.

The next day, rinse the hock, place in a saucepan with water to cover, bring to the boil, then drain. Cook in fresh water with a bay leaf either in a pressure-cooker with ¾ pint of water, for 25–30 minutes, or in a saucepan, with water to cover, for an hour or two. Drain off but keep the water. Once cool, skin and bone the hock and either mince the meat or cut it into small pieces.

Mix the meat with the drained split peas and put into an oven-proof dish with enough of the water in which the hock was cooked to almost cover. Add a good knob or two of butter and some pepper (there should be still be enough salt in the meat). Cover and bake in a medium oven for half an hour or more until the split peas are cooked, checking the moisture content once in a while.

The saffron colours of this dish are a delight.

YOU WILL NEED:

Smoked bacon hock
Yellow split peas
Bay leaf
Butter
Pepper

Yorkshire Asparagussed Chops

The very title has almost told you the recipe and how to do it.

Using a shallow baking pan or enamelled iron pot, bake chops (lamb or pork) in a medium oven, until they are three-quarters cooked. Turn up the heat. Strain off most of the fat. Surround the meat with cooked asparagus tips, fresh or canned, and coat them with a thin layer of Yorkshire pudding mix (see p. 184).

Return the dish to a hot oven for about 30 minutes. The cooking can also be accomplished under the grill.

YOU WILL NEED:

Lamb or pork chops
Asparagus tips
Yorkshire pudding batter

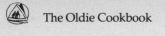

Barbecued Belly Strips

This is a fine, cheap and tasty dish for a winter's evening.

Cut, or ask the butcher to cut, 1-inch slices of lean belly pork, bones 'n' all. Pare off the skin with a very sharp knife, elevating the blade towards the skin as you separate it from the meat.

Make a paste of 5 parts tomato ketchup to 1 part Worcestershire sauce, 1 teaspoon of chilli-con-carne powder and salt. Coat the meat all over with this colourful sauce and allow to marinate for an hour or two or overnight.

At least half an hour before you start to cook the meat, put peppered and salted halved potatoes on to an oven shelf, and, in a roasting tin, the pork skin, cut into strips, salted and oiled.

Place the strips of marinated meat in a fireproof dish and bake in a medium oven, or grill them slowly, until cooked. Either method will take an hour or more as they need to be well done. Pour off and discard all fat shed from meat and skins.

You will now have baked potatoes and barbecued strips for your meal and, as a bonus, some fine crackling to be eaten hot or cold with drinks. (The crackling may need further cooking in a very hot oven.)

YOU WILL NEED:

Belly pork
Tomato ketchup
Worcestershire sauce

Chilli-con-carne powder
Salt and pepper
Potatoes

Pork and Cider

This delicious stew is quick and simple to make.

Cut up, into pieces of an edible size, equal quantities of loin or other lean cut of pork, well-washed leeks and peeled potatoes.

Melt some butter in a pressure cooker, fireproof pot or oven casserole. Throw in the ingredients with pepper and salt and stir around for a while. Shake a tablespoon or so of flour over the contents of the pot and stir again. Add cider to almost cover. Pressure cook for 20 minutes, or simmer, covered, on the stove for about an hour, or cook, again covered, in a moderate oven for the same length of time.

A few Jerusalem artichokes are a great addition to the pot, if they do not give you the wind!

YOU WILL NEED:

Pork
Leeks
Potatoes
Jerusalem artichokes (optional)

Butter
Flour
Pepper and salt
Cider

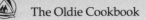

Pork Chops Vinaigrette

This is both an 'every-day' and a party dish. It seldom fails to please. Served with baked potatoes in their skins, the combination of temperatures, tastes and textures is a winner.

Fry pork chops or, better still, bake them in the oven.

Make an elaborate vinaigrette with olive oil (only a little oil), vinegar, pepper and salt, finely chopped onion, shallot or chives, capers, chopped parsley or other fresh herb, diced gherkin, slivers of black or green olives, green peppercorns and/or whatever else you think may add zest.

As soon as the chops are cooked, cover with the cold vinaigrette, and serve immediately with halved baked potatoes. The plain potato flesh provides a happy buffer to the other tastes and textures.

You will need:

Pork chops
Potatoes
An elaborate vinaigrette

Balkan Veal Stew

Here is a stew that is simple to make and exotic to taste.

Heat about 2 tablespoons of olive oil in a saucepan. Add 2 chopped onions, 1 chopped clove of garlic, pepper and salt, 3 bay leaves and 12 juniper berries. Cook slowly until the onion becomes transparent. Now add stewing veal cut into edible-sized pieces and a heaped teaspoon of flour. Stir around and continue to cook for a little longer. Pour in liquid made up of half dry white wine and half stock to almost cover the meat.

Simmer gently with the lid on for half an hour. Complete the cooking (another 20–25 minutes) uncovered to reduce the liquid content and concentrate the taste. Extract the bay leaves.

Garnish the veal with a little chopped parsley and serve with rice.

YOU WILL NEED:
Chopped stewing veal
Olive oil
Onions
Garlic
Bay leaves
Juniper berries
Pepper and salt
Flour
Dry white wine
Stock
Parsley

Chicken and Coriander Seeds

Buy chicken breasts (or cut them from a chicken), tear off the skin and pare away and discard any bone or gristle. Cut each breast into 4 strips. One breast from a large chicken should do for 2 people.

In a bowl make a vinaigrette (see p. 67), adding dry mustard, pepper and salt, and some 40–50 lightly-crushed coriander seeds (break them up with a pestle and mortar or crush a few at a time with the back of a wooden spoon in a bowl). Marinate the pieces of chicken in this mixture for from a few hours to overnight, turning them occasionally.

Fry the chicken slowly in the marinade until it is well cooked and golden brown. Arrange on a serving plate and keep hot.

Add a little flour to what remains in the pan. Cook for just a moment longer and then stir in some dry white wine or stock. Scrape the pan drippings free and cook until the sauce thickens. Pour over the chicken and serve with vegetables of your choice.

You will need:

Chicken breasts
Vinaigrette
Dry mustard
Coriander seeds
Flour
Dry white wine or stock

Chicken on Swede

Here is a cheap and rustic dish, elevated to dinner party status by a spirited addition.

Allow 2 chicken thighs per person, boned (but not skinned) and rolled into bundles. If you bone them yourself, keep the bones and throw them in with the swede while it is cooking. Pare away the outer skin of a swede or more. Cut the flesh into smallish cubes or slices. Cover with water or stock (add the thigh bones) and boil for 15–30 minutes, or until soft. Pour off the cooking water for a later-to-be-enjoyed soup (see p. 55) and extract the bones. Mash the swede with butter, pepper and salt. Now stir in a measure of ouzo, Pernod, Ricard, or other aniseed spirit.

Cover the bottom of an ovenproof dish with the mashed swede and arrange the chicken thighs on top. Dribble or brush a little olive oil over each. Add salt, and a good milling of black pepper from the pepper mill. If it is more convenient, the preparation so far can be done well in advance.

Bake the dish in a medium to hot oven for 1½ hours, or longer. Anyhow, after the chicken skin has become crisp and golden the dish will be ready for the table.

That's it. And it is a stunner. Serve with baked or mashed potato, or beans, or a salad, or . . .

YOU WILL NEED:

Swede
Stock (optional)
Butter
Pepper and salt
Ouzo or another aniseed spirit
Chicken thighs
Olive oil
Milled pepper

A Quick Chicken Stew

Pour a pint of stock (with a little dry white wine if desired) into a pressure cooker or saucepan. Throw in a handful of washed pearl barley. Add plenty of sliced carrots, half a washed, de-pipped lemon and pepper and salt. Now lay a chicken on top and pressure cook for 20 minutes if it is a roaster, or 25 minutes for a boiler. If you are using a saucepan cover and simmer gently for 1–1½ hours on the stove.

Once cooked, lift out the chicken (discard the lemon) and place on a serving dish. Thicken the juices with a little cornflour mixed with cold water then pour this around the chicken with the carrots and pearl barley. The chicken should almost fall apart with the aid of a spoon and fork.

YOU WILL NEED:

Chicken
Stock (with a little white wine if desired)
Pearl barley
Carrots

Lemon
Pepper and salt
Cornflour

White Chicken Breast and Peppers

This is a simple dish where the colours and flavours are clear and strong.

Heat about 2 table-spoons of olive oil in a frying-pan. Add de-pipped and finely-chopped sweet red peppers (allow 1 for 2 people), pressed garlic, a few cumquats, finely-cut (no pips), grated fresh ginger root to taste, pepper and salt. Cover and cook slowly until the peppers are soft.

Gently poach the chicken breasts (allow 1 per person) in stock with a couple of bay leaves for 15–20 minutes, timed so that they will be ready when wanted (you can leave them in the stock to keep hot for a while).

When you are ready for this dish, lift the hot chicken breasts from their stock (good for soup) and place them in a serving dish or on individual plates. Cover them with the cooked peppers in their sauce. Offer a bowl of boiled rice as an accompaniment.

YOU WILL NEED:

Chicken breasts	Garlic
Stock	Cumquats
Bay leaves	Ginger root
Olive oil	Pepper and salt
Red peppers	Rice

The Oldie Cookbook

Chicken with Carrots

This is a colourful and simple way to cook a chicken. It is distinctive and quite delicious.

Take a whole chicken, or parts of one, and fry in olive oil until lightly browned. Then place in a fireproof pot or pressure cooker.

In a large wine glass make a paste with a level teaspoon of turmeric powder and a little dry white wine. Top up the glass with more wine. Stir well and pour the mixture over the chicken. If your wine glass is small, add another measure, or two, of wine – or water. Throw in a chopped onion and completely smother the chicken with roundels of carrot. Add salt and mill over plenty of black pepper.

Cover and cook slowly for 1½ hours on top of the stove, in a moderate oven, or for 25 minutes in the pressure cooker.

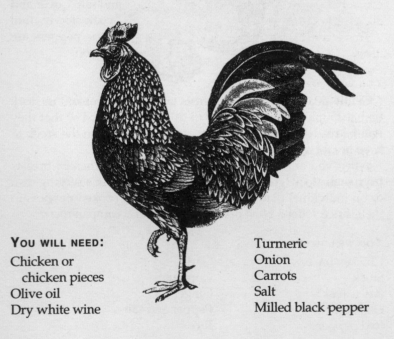

YOU WILL NEED:
Chicken or
  chicken pieces
Olive oil
Dry white wine

Turmeric
Onion
Carrots
Salt
Milled black pepper

Chicken and Potatoes

Here is a dish that takes some beating for simplicity, speed and ease of preparation. You will need a deepish, lidded frying pan – an electric one will do well.

Cut the breasts off a chicken (dissect the remainder for a curry, see p. 116), or buy chicken breasts. Cut the breasts (skin, too, if you like) into bite-sized pieces.

Heat around 2 tablespoons of olive oil in a frying-pan. Fry a finely-chopped onion until brown (this gives the dish some colour and extra taste). Add 1–2 lb. of diced potatoes (unpeeled if you are in a hurry), then the chicken pieces. Season with pepper and salt and throw in some chopped herb of your choice, fresh or dried.

Stir it all around, put the lid on the frying pan, and cook slowly (frying/steaming) for about ¾ of an hour, or until the potatoes are cooked through – turning everything around every so often. That's all.

This is a peasanty, tasty, glowingly-golden dish – complete in itself.

YOU WILL NEED:

Chicken breasts
Onion
Potatoes
A fresh or dried herb
Olive oil
Pepper and salt

Kok o'California

It was not easy to buy fresh herbs in New Haven, Connecticut in 1969. It was also rather difficult to dispose of disposable baby's nappies (diapers). However, the minute apartment where we lived had a large balcony, so, with containers bought from the Salvation Army, subsoil sand gleaned from a nearby building site and soiled nappies, I was able to create a very fine garden of flowers, vegetables and herbs. The *bouquet garni* for this recipe came from my 'garden'.

The age-range of chickens offered for sale in the United States is far more varied than in Europe. 'Fryers' were originally used for this recipe, but any chicken will do. Should you want a more robust dish, Halal butchers nearly always stock large cockerels at a reasonable price and will skin and cut up the bird for you.

Marinate the pieces of an old or young bird for hours to days in red wine to cover (Californian for preference), *bouquet garni* (or fresh herbs tied together in a couple of bay leaves), chopped onion, pepper, salt, a dash of olive oil and a little gravy browning.

Extract the pieces of chicken from the marinade, dab them dry and dip them into a mixture of flour, salt and pepper. Heat some butter and oil in a saucepan and in it brown plenty of sliced garlic. Throw in the chicken pieces and cook until the meat has begun to change colour. If there is a little of the seasoned flour left over, add this to the pan. Now just cover the meat with the marinade, topping up with more red wine to cover if necessary. Throw in a handful of very small button mushrooms (best from a can) and a generous amount of stoned black olives (½ lb. would be the maximum).

Cover the pan and cook the chicken very gently on the top of the stove for 1–2 hours, depending on the size and age of the bird. Alternatively, you can cook it in a slow oven which is just as good, if not better.

For those pressed for time, this entire dish, having been marinated for a day or two beforehand, can be completed, from the frying garlic stage onwards in a pressure cooker in 15–30 minutes, again depending on the nature of the bird.

When the chicken is cooked, spoon off any fat from the surface and extract the *bouquet garni*. If you think the juices should be thicker, add a little cornflour mixed with cold water and cook for a little longer.

Serve the Kok o'California with mashed or new potatoes. The aromatic flavours transform what is a very simple dish.

YOU WILL NEED:

Chicken or cockerel	Gravy browning
Bouquet garni	Garlic
Onion	Mushrooms
Flour	Black olives (stoned)
Pepper and salt	Cornflour
Olive oil and butter	

Chicken Leftovers

A glorious way of using up cooked chicken leftovers – or any other meat for that matter – is to mince it finely (skin 'n' all) with a small piece of lemon, less pips. Don't overdo the lemon as it can dominate the taste. Put a slice or two of bread through the mincer at the finish to make sure that all the chicken meat is expelled.

Mix your mince with a beaten egg, pepper and salt and a little flour to reach a firm but tacky consistency. Form this mix into bite-sized balls, roll them in flour and fry in oil until they are browning and heated through. Shake the pan often to make sure the balls roll and cook fairly evenly.

Serve plain with rice. They also go down very well with drinks.

YOU WILL NEED:

Chicken or other meat leftovers
Lemon
Egg
Pepper and salt
Flour
Cooking oil

Chicken and Lemon Beans

You can use virtually any dried beans for this excellent dish although I think pinto beans are best.

Soak the beans for several hours beforehand (or overnight). Put a chicken in a heavy cooking-pot or pressure cooker and surround with the drained beans. Add stock, or water and a stock cube to just cover the beans, and salt and pepper.

Put a well-scrubbed whole lemon on the beans, then either pressure cook for about 20 minutes (more or less, depending upon the age and size of the bird) or, if using a pot, boil rapidly for 10 minutes then turn down the heat and cook slowly on the stove or in a very moderate oven for 1½–2 hours until the chicken is cooked and the beans tender.

Melt a good ounce of butter in a saucepan and stir in a tablespoon of flour to form a paste. When the chicken and beans are cooked, lift the bird on to a serving dish, discard the lemon and strain the liquid from the pan (keep the beans in the pot) into the flour and butter paste. Whisk up over a gentle heat to form a creamy sauce, then pour over the beans and cook for a little longer.

Now either add the thickened beans to surround the chicken in its serving dish, or carve the bird, arrange in a dish and spoon the beans over the top.

What remains (if any) will make a splendid soup – even better if you boil up any remaining bones and skin for the stock.

You will need:

Chicken
Dried beans
Water or stock
Lemon
Pepper and salt
Butter
Flour

Chicken Curries

Heat a tablespoon each of oil and butter in a saucepan or oven-proof pot. Gently fry a chopped onion and 3–4 crushed cloves of garlic until they become transparent.

Make a paste of a tablespoon of curry powder, a little salt, a crumbled stock cube perhaps, a pinch of sugar, a dash of vinegar and water. Combine this with the onions and garlic and keep stirring for a while over the heat.

Add chicken joints (or a chicken you have jointed) and turn them around until they are nicely coated, then stir in a can of chopped tomatoes. Cover the pan and cook very slowly on the stove or in a moderate oven for up to an hour. You will then have made an excellent curry.

Now, just to make it known to yourself and to anyone else that you can also make a completely different chicken curry, try this one:

Start as before but use about 3 times as much onion (adding more garlic will not make a great deal of difference). To the softened onions and garlic add a level teaspoonful of turmeric powder, a small piece of cinnamon stick, 5–6 cardamoms, the same number of cloves, a little ginger powder or some grated fresh ginger root (peeled), salt, and that touch of sugar and vinegar that seems to make so much difference. Cook these spices gently for a little while to release the oils and aromas. Add the chicken pieces and coat well with the mixture. Stir in a little stock this time, in place of the tomatoes, and cook as before.

Serve these dishes with rice.

There are plenty of other ingredients you can add to alter the taste of a basic curry dish: fenugreek seeds, or the leaves (known as methi leaves), with their highly distinctive flavour, bay leaf, asafoetida, fresh chillies or chilli powder, English dry mustard, star aniseed, coriander seeds or leaves, cumin, peppercorns, paprika, creamed coconut and peanut butter are some.

Note: When roasting a chicken that may be too large for one meal, it is an idea to cut off the legs and thighs and cook these as a curry in the oven at the same time, to eat later or freeze.

YOU WILL NEED:

Chicken
Onion
Garlic
Butter
Oil
Salt
Sugar
Vinegar
Curry powder
Canned tomatoes
Stock cube (optional)

IN ADDITION FOR THE SECOND CURRY:

Turmeric
Cloves
Cardamoms
Cinnamon
Ginger
Stock

Chicken and Black-eyed Beans

This ridiculously easy main course can be started in the morning, forgotten about all day then cooked in a few minutes in the evening, using a pressure cooker. It can also be accomplished in the oven or slowly in a pot on the top of the stove but will, of course, take longer.

Put a packet of black-eyed beans to soak in plenty of cold water first thing in the morning.

In the evening, put a chicken (chicken pieces will do but they won't look as impressive on the serving dish) in your pressure cooker or cooking pot and surround with the drained, soaked beans. Add a few crushed cloves of garlic, pepper and salt, then pour in water (with a chicken stock cube if desired) to just cover the beans.

Depending upon the size of the chicken and on whether it is

whole or jointed, pressure-cook for 15–30 minutes. Alternatively, cover your pot and boil quickly for 10 minutes then stew gently on the stove or in a moderate oven for ¾–1½ hours.

When cooked, lift out the chicken and keep it warm. Thicken the bean sauce with a little potato flour, or cornflour, that has been mixed in cold water and cook for a bit longer.

Serve by placing the chicken on a dish and surrounding it with the beans. Some chopped parsley over all will delight the eye. Anything left over will become the start of a soup.

YOU WILL NEED:
Chicken or chicken pieces
Black-eyed beans
Garlic
Pepper and salt
Chicken stock cube (optional)
Potato flour or cornflour.
Parsley

Boned Christmas Turkey (and some spin-offs)

Never again will I cook a Christmas turkey without boning it first. Slicing up a bird with its bones in place is a tricky operation for most carvers, whereas a boned stuffed turkey may be cut across from either end (for brown or white meat) with the utmost simplicity.

You may be able to persuade a butcher to bone the bird for you. Otherwise follow the direction below. It does take time, at least an hour, but I promise you that it will be worth it.

You will need a stiff and very sharp kitchen knife (which should be resharpened occasionally during the operation).

Cut off the 2 outer joints from each wing, the Pope's Nose, and if you want to make it easier, the drumsticks. Now, make an incision from neck to tail down the back of the bird and, holding the skin and flesh with one hand slowly cut the meat away from the carcass.

A difficulty will occur when you reach the point where the thigh-bone joins the main frame at a tight ball socket. Carefully pull/break the thigh-bone from the carcass and pare the meat away from it (and from the drumsticks if you left them attached), so that eventually you can extract the bones.

The wing bone is easier to cut from the carcass and can be separated from its meat by running the blade all around it. Extract the wishbone.

Be very careful not to break the skin when you come to the ridge of the breast-bone. Work towards it then cut between breast-bone and skin, easing the carcass and skin apart as you do so.

Lay your boned, spread-eagled turkey skin side down and place the stuffing on top from head to tail (see pp. 182–3 for stuffings). Depending on its size you will need 2–3 lb. of stuffing to 'fill' the

MERRY
XMAS

Watehhouse.

bird. Stitch up your original incision with string, or use a kebab skewer. Sew up any gaps where stuffing might escape. Turn the bird over and pat it as nearly as possible into its original shape. It is now ready for the roasting tin. All this may be done the day before Christmas, but the bird must be kept cool.

With this operation complete, you can make a stock. Throw all the bones (you may have to crash through the carcass with a meat axe to break it up a bit), giblets (less liver), Pope's nose and other debris, into a saucepan. Add a well scrubbed pig's trotter, bay leaf, chopped onion, a clove or two of garlic, pepper and salt. Cover with cold water and either pressure cook for 35–40 minutes or simmer slowly for 2 or more hours. (You can leave it in the bottom oven of an Aga for 24 hours.) The strained stock can be used for the gravy, soup or simply frozen as stock.

Now, you can either freeze the wings and drumsticks as they are (if you removed them), or if you bought a frozen turkey, extract the meat from the bones, cut it up and make a curry (see p. 116) which, once cooked, can then be frozen.

Finally, take the liver and cut it into small pieces. Put a morsel at the end of a very thinly-sliced rasher of smoked streaky bacon and roll it up. Secure the roll by spearing it with a wooden toothpick. Repeat the operation to use up all the liver. Fry these rolls and enjoy them hot with drinks.

In a couple of hours, you will have formed a boned, stuffed turkey, made a delicious curry, brewed up a splendid stock and made some 'gobblers on horseback'. That's what I call a job well done before Christmas. Whoever performs the operation deserves a glass of Champagne – at least!

You will need:

A turkey
Stuffings
Onion, garlic, bay leaf, pepper and salt
A pig's trotter
Rashers of thinly-sliced, smoked streaky bacon
Wooden toothpicks
Spices for a curry

Lamb and Courgettes

In the summertime, when courgettes and lamb are plentiful, a very simple and successful dish may be made as follows.

Take a piece, or pieces, of lamb, hogget or mutton. A boned joint is better but the cheaper bony cuts from the scrag end and middle will do perfectly well. Pare off the surplus fat before putting the meat into a covered pan, lidded electric frying pan, casserole or close-covered pot. Surround with cut-up courgettes, adding a couple of peeled and crushed cloves of garlic, a small sprig of rosemary, pepper and salt and a splash of cider.

Cover and cook this dish very slowly for 1, 2 or even 3 hours, depending on the meat involved. Check it every so often to see that there is still moisture in the pot. If not, add a little more cider. (You will want very little moisture at the end.) Extract the rosemary sprig before you serve this excellent combination of meat and vegetable. Relying more on taste than looks for its success, a sprinkling of chopped parsley over the top before serving is a good idea.

With a little forethought and very little preparation time or trouble involved, this informal dish will be ready no matter when it is required.

YOU WILL NEED:

A piece or pieces of lamb or mutton
Courgettes
Garlic
Rosemary
Pepper and salt
Cider
Parsley

Lamb and Beans

This simple main course appears frequently on my table.

Soak a packet of haricot beans in cold water for 12 hours or more.

Take the lower or upper half of a leg of lamb (or mutton), remove all excess fat and place in a cooking pot or pressure cooker. Drain the soaked beans and tip them in. Add a couple of bay leaves, a clove of garlic and some pepper and salt. Cover it all with water and boil rapidly for 10 minutes, then simmer on the stove (lid on) or in a moderate oven for 1–1½ hours, depending on the size and age of the joint. Alternatively, pressure cook for 25–30 minutes.

When cooked , lift out the joint and if it is the lower half of the leg, hold it upright by the exposed bone, and carve downwards all around. Serve with the beans and sprinkle with a little chopped parsley.

Any leftover juice and beans will make an excellent soup.

You will need:

The lower or upper half of a leg of lamb or mutton
Haricot beans
Bay leaves
Garlic
Pepper and salt
Parsley

Drunken Lamb Stew

This dish uses breast of lamb which is a cheap but fatty cut. It is therefore best cooked a day in advance and then chilled so that any fat will rise to the surface and can be removed easily before reheating.

Chop up an onion and throw it into your stewpot or pressure cooker. On top of this place a thick layer of breast of lamb (about 2 lb.) cut into smallish pieces by the butcher. Dust over some flour and add a can of mushrooms with the brine, and about ¼ lb. of smoked streaky bacon cut into small pieces. As there will be enough salt in the brine and bacon, just add pepper.

Pour in enough dry white wine to reach the top of the meat, then cover with medium-sized whole peeled potatoes.

Cook slowly on top of the stove until you think that the meat will fall from the bone (2 hours or more) or for 30 minutes in the pressure cooker. This is a fine dish for a winter's evening.

YOU WILL NEED:

Onion	Smoked streaky bacon
Breast of lamb	Pepper
Flour	Dry white wine
Can of mushrooms	Potatoes

Pheasant or Pork in Cabbage

Here is a classic example of a party dish that 'looks after itself', thus giving the host or hostess plenty of time for other things. Even an ancient pheasant will become mouth-wateringly tender as it slowly steams in the moisture content of the cabbage.

Try to leave some of the cabbage behind in the pot at the end of the meal. This will make a wonderful basis for soup.

Pork will take the place of a pheasant, but it will no longer be quite such an elegant dish. Hocks, trotters, lean belly and other non-fatty lesser cuts are the best pieces to use.

Chop a large, dark green cabbage (January King is best) into small pieces (you may also use spinach, chard, sprout tops, halved Brussels sprouts, beetroot tops, or a mixture of any or all). Throw these into a deep iron casserole.

Add, say, half a glass of dry white wine and half that amount of olive oil. No more liquid will be necessary as the moisture from the leaves will provide all that is required. Season with milled pepper and salt.

Now, with your hands, turn the chopped greens over and over until they glisten. Make a 'nest' in the shiny greenery, and in it

place the pheasant, or pork. Surround this with medium-sized whole, peeled potatoes.

Cover the pot tightly and cook in a low to medium oven for 2½–3 hours. If the bird is not obviously overcooked, raise the heat shortly before you come to serve this splendid dish. This action will help to crispen the cabbage pieces that touch the sides of the pot, adding extra tastes and smells (especially to the soup that you will be making later).

The fine, rich smell of this dish as it cooks is very penetrating.

YOU WILL NEED:
Pheasant, or pork hocks, trotters or belly
Dark green cabbage or any other greens
Dry white wine
Olive oil
Salt and milled pepper
Potatoes

A Pheasant under Pressure

Friends and acquaintances of marksmen or poachers are sometimes presented in wintertime with a gift of a fully feathered pheasant. With the grateful recipient reluctant to hang, pluck and truss the object, and butchers also unwilling to offer their services, what is the solution? Do it yourself in the following easy if slightly wasteful manner:

With a sharp knife cut through the feathers down either side of the breast bone. Peel back skin and feathers in one and pare away the breast meat. Now, what you do with the rest depends on you. Throw it away, skin more meat to add to game pies, or skin and boil the carcass, stringy legs and wings to make concentrated game stock – the choice is yours.

125

Cut the breast meat into smallish pieces extracting any shot. Heat an ounce or so of butter in a pressure cooker or fireproof pot. Throw in chopped leeks (1–2 per person) and cook gently for a short time, then stir in a good tablespoon of flour, and season with pepper and salt.

Add the pheasant pieces, a handful of stoned black olives and the juice of ¼ lemon. Cook for a little longer, then pour in half and half stock and dry white wine to just cover. Cover the pot and cook in a low oven, or simmer very gently on the stove for 1–1½ hours, or pressure cook for 15 minutes.

Serve with mashed potatoes.

YOU WILL NEED:

Pheasant
Leeks
Flour
Pepper and salt
Black olives
Lemon
Stock
Dry white wine

Pheasant Stew

Here is a festive dish that, using only the breast meat, can be easily handled at the table by both the very young and very old. Anyway, a dish that does not involve bones is an asset at any party.

Take an under-hung pheasant or two. If they are still feathered, follow the procedure in the preceeding recipe.

Cut the breast meat into small pieces and marinate them in red wine for a few hours. This preparation has the advantage of enabling you to locate and extract shot comparatively easily.

Drain and dip the pieces of meat in flour, pepper and salt. Heat a tablespoon or two of butter in a heavy fireproof pot and gently frizzle the pheasant for a short time. Stir in a little more of the seasoned flour. Cook for a minute or two then pour in the marinating liquid, stirring over the heat all the time. Add more red wine if you think it is necessary and a little gravy browning to enrich the appearance.

Put a lid on the pot and cook in a medium oven for 25–30 minutes.

Do not add any strong 'extras' such as herbs or port, as one of the pleasures of this dish is that it is delicate and not too gamey. Serve with mashed or baked potatoes, and a green salad with a sharp dressing.

YOU WILL NEED:

Pheasant
Red wine
Flour
Pepper and salt
Butter
Gravy browning

Hare

Hare is usually cooked to such a degree of richness and served with so many chipped and sharp bones that you are not too keen on eating a second until the memory of the first is long forgotten.

If you are up to dealing with it, bone your hare (this is not nearly as difficult as you would expect), cut the meat into edible-sized pieces and dip in seasoned flour. Heat around 2 tablespoons of olive or vegetable oil (not butter) in a cooking pot and fry the meat for a short while. Add plenty of stoned, green olives, then pour in half a bottle of dry white wine (not red). Cover and cook slowly on the stove or in a medium oven for an hour or more, until the meat is tender.

Serve with mashed potato and one plain boiled vegetable, such as carrots.

YOU WILL NEED:

Hare
Flour
Pepper and salt
Oil
Green olives
Dry white wine

A Whole Liver (baked or stuffed)

There are two good recipes for a whole lamb's liver.

The first is simply to press slices of garlic into slanted cuts made in the liver, then lay it in a shallow fireproof dish, grind black pepper over the top and cover it completely with thin slices of smoked streaky bacon. Pour a little dry white wine around its base and grill it or bake it in a moderate oven for about 20 minutes.

The following recipe takes this dish a little further, turning it into more of a party dish by stuffing the liver.

Lay the whole liver on a board and with a very sharp knife slice it *almost* through horizontally. Into this cavity place a mixture of about ½ lb. of minced veal, a beaten egg, a little flour, 2–3 cloves of crushed garlic, chopped sage leaves, pepper and salt.

Pat the liver into a regular shape, place it in an oven-proof dish and cover well with thinly sliced smoked streaky bacon. Pour round a little white wine and bake for ¾–1 hour.

Cut the stuffed liver into 1-inch slices and serve with a green salad.

YOU WILL NEED:

Whole lamb's liver
Garlic
Pepper
Smoked streaky bacon
Dry white wine

FOR THE STUFFING:

Minced veal
Garlic
Egg
Flour
Sage
Pepper and salt

129

Crispy Rare Liver

This dish can be prepared well before it is wanted at the table. As liver cooks in so short a time, you can rise from the table and return with your masterpiece in no time at all. Here is what you can do in advance:

Prepare the liver (calf's or lamb's) by removing all stringy tissue, then cut into edible-sized pieces and set aside. Chop up rashers of streaky bacon (2–3 per person), a good handful of parsley and some garlic cloves. Fry these in a little olive oil until they are all crisp and brown. Take the pan off the heat and pour off any excess fat.

When you are ready to eat, heat up the pan with the bacony mix in it and when very hot, throw in the liver pieces (having drained any liquid that the liver may have given off in the meantime). Stir and turn all around constantly. The cooking will only take a minute or two – longer than that and the liver will toughen and ruin the dish. Take the pan off the heat immediately the liver is cooked. Mill over some black pepper (there should be enough salt from the bacon, but test) and serve. This will only take a minute or two.

YOU WILL NEED:
Liver (calf's or lamb's)
Olive oil
Bacon
Parsley
Garlic
Milled pepper

Tangley Liver and Bacon

This variation on a classic dish takes very little time to prepare and cook, maintains a pleasant combination of tastes and texture, and makes a fine presentation.

Cut rashers of smoked streaky bacon (allow 2–3 per person) into small slivers and fry until crisp. Extract them from the fat and place on absorbent kitchen paper before spreading them evenly on the bottom of an iron or other fireproof dish.

Cut lamb's liver into strips. Lay these (crossing over each other) on top of the bacon. Sprinkle a little best olive oil over all and give a good milling of black pepper over the top (there will be enough salt from the bacon). Place beneath a slow grill until the liver is just cooked (5–10 minutes).

The result will be a kind of pancake. Slice and serve hot with a generous amount of chopped parsley.

YOU WILL NEED:

Smoked streaky bacon
Lamb's liver
Olive oil
Black pepper
Parsley

Kidneys

Fresh lambs' kidneys recently extracted from their fat are best. As a general rule, thinly-sliced lambs' kidneys should be cooked quickly for a short time. Ox kidney is best cooked slowly for much longer and should be left in salted water for a while beforehand.

Kidneys and Kasha

Skin, core and thinly slice lambs' kidneys. Allow them to rest in some dry white wine with pepper, salt and a bay leaf while the kasha is cooking.

Fry a handful or two of brown kasha (buckwheat) in oil until the grain begins to smell nicely. Add pepper and salt and just cover with stock or water. Cook very slowly in a covered pan on top of the stove or in an earthenware pot in a slow oven for an hour or so. Check occasionally to see if a little more liquid is needed. Taste a sample as you go along.

When the kasha is tender, having absorbed the water, put the kidneys and their marinade in a saucepan and cook for 5–10 minutes. When they are done, thicken the liquid with a touch of cornflour or potato flour (mixed with a little cold water) and simmer for a little longer.

Arrange the kidneys with the kasha on a dish and serve with a green salad.

YOU WILL NEED:
Kidneys
Dry white wine
Kasha (buckwheat)
Oil
Pepper and salt
Stock or water

Ox Kidney

Take a whole, or part of an ox kidney. Divide it horizontally and discard the fatty tissue that runs its length, or in the winter, feed it to your wild birds. Cut the kidney into edible-sized pieces, paring away any more fat, and rinse in salted water.

Now, in a pan that can be covered, fry a chopped onion gently in butter. When this is transparent, but not brown in any way, add the kidney, a bay leaf, pepper and salt. Cook for just a little while, and then add a sprinkling of flour. Keep turning the pieces around. Now pour in red wine to reach about half to three-quarters of the way up the solids. A small dash of tomato ketchup added at this stage is to the advantage of the dish. Put the lid on the pan and cook the kidneys slowly on the stove or in a low oven for ½–1 hour.

Sprinkle with chopped parsley and serve with French bread, mashed potato, or rice.

YOU WILL NEED:

An ox kidney – or part of one
Butter
Onion
Bay leaf
Pepper and salt

Flour
Red wine
Tomato ketchup
Parsley

Kids in Skins

Pare away the excess fat from lambs' kidneys leaving them still encased in a thin layer. Be careful not to cut into, and thus through the kidney skin. Put the kidneys in a shallow roasting pan and bake, with potatoes in their skins, in a medium to hot oven.

The potatoes, spiked to prevent them from bursting, will take 1½–2 hours to cook (depending on size), the kidneys a little less time.

Pepper and salt the halved potatoes and serve the kidneys on top so that any juices will soak deliciously into them.

Kidneys baked in this way will keep moist and succulent. Most of the fat will have melted off by the time they are cooked, leaving them with a lovely crispy coating.

Add the hot fat and escaped juices to your dripping pot.

YOU WILL NEED:

Lambs' kidneys in their fat
Potatoes
Salt and pepper

JON. CRAMER.

Kids 'n' Crumbs

In this presentation, the combination of two heats, two tastes and two textures is a simple delight.

Halve, skin, core and thinly slice lambs' kidneys. Cook them in butter in a pan, or place them under the grill.

Fry breadcrumbs slowly in butter and oil with plenty of pepper and salt. They can burn easily, so keep stirring and turning them over until they are crisp and golden brown.

When the kidneys are just cooked, throw them with their juices on to warm plates. Cover with the sizzling crumbs and serve with a little chopped parsley on top if possible.

YOU WILL NEED:
Lambs' kidneys
Breadcrumbs
Butter and oil
Pepper and salt
Parsley

Bold and Simple Kidneys

Every lover of offal should know this dish. It is wonderfully delicious and takes so little time to make.

Halve, core, skin and thinly slice lamb's kidneys. Heat some butter and oil mixed in a frying pan. Add a bay leaf. Throw in the kidney slices and add pepper and salt. Cook quickly until the blood stops flowing. This will not take long. Extract the bay leaf.

Sprinkle a teaspoon or so of flour over the kidneys and their juices. Stir this in and cook for just a little while longer. Now add a glassful of dry white wine and simmer until the sauce thickens. Serve immediately with a sprinkling of chopped parsley on top.

For a more substantial dish, serve with rice.

YOU WILL NEED:
Lamb's kidneys
Butter and oil
Bay leaf
Pepper and salt
Flour
Dry white wine
Parsley

Lucky Dip Fish

This dish can be made grand or simple depending on the type of fish you use. Either way it is delicious.

    Take a mixture of white fish, such as cod, haddock, monkfish or the like, and uncooked shellfish of any kind, such as mussels,

shrimps, scallops, etc. Previously cooked shellfish (avoid brined and pickled) should be added later. Choose the ingredients to suit your purse.

Make some mashed potato, on the dry side.

Place the uncooked seafood in a saucepan with milk and water to just cover. Add a bay leaf, pepper, salt and a few knobs of butter. Bring the liquid to a very gentle boil and poach the fish for 5 minutes. Then lift out the seafood and remove any skin, shells and bones.

Now make a thick white sauce (p. 64), using the strained milky liquid in which the fish were poached. When this is cooked, throw in some finely chopped mushrooms. A few sweet-corn kernels also make an excellent addition.

Place all the seafood in individual fireproof bowls, deep scallop shells or a pie dish, and cover with the white sauce containing mushrooms and sweet corn. Gently amalgamate fish and sauce. Top with mashed potato.

Bake or slowly grill the dish or dishes until the 'lucky dip' is browning on top and the inside piping hot. This will take up to 30 minutes depending on the size of the dish.

YOU WILL NEED:

White fish
Shellfish
Milk
Pepper and salt
Bay leaf
White sauce
Mushrooms
Sweet corn
Mashed potato

Baked Trout

Buy a trout (with glistening eye) for each person. Cut off the heads and tails, then gut them, not forgetting to scrape away the dark vessel that runs down inside the ridge of the body cavity. Stuff some heads or fronds of fresh or dried dill into the cavity of each trout then lay them in a flat oven-proof dish or tray with 2 lemon slices on top, with a knob or two of butter. Sprinkle salt over all.

Place under a slow grill until they are cooked right through (10–15 minutes), then turn up the heat to crispen the skin. There is no need to turn the fish over. Serve with their juices.

YOU WILL NEED:

Trout
Dill
Lemon
Butter
Salt

Tuna Fishcake

Here is a simple one. This dish will please children as well as adults – and that is not always easy.

Make some well-seasoned mashed potato (see p. 77). Add the drained contents of a can of tuna fish. (The proportion of potato to tuna should be roughly 3 to 1.) Cut the tuna into the potato finely, but do not mash it. Check the seasoning. The addition of some finely-chopped parsley will do wonders.

Coat the surface of a frying pan with a little olive (or other) oil, dripping or butter. Add your tunny-spud mixture. Spread it out evenly, and cook slowly until heated through and a light brown crust has formed on the bottom.

It is ready as it is, but you may want to turn it over to brown the other side. Serve like a cake, cut into sections. Those with children will know that tomato ketchup is almost an obligatory supplement.

YOU WILL NEED:

Mashed potato
Canned tuna
Parsley (optional)
Oil, dripping or butter

Eggs and Toms

The salivary glands flow when this bubbling and most delicious-smelling dish is offered at the table.

Take a fireproof serving dish and cover the bottom with a layer of sliced fresh tomatoes (canned ones will do but first strain off the juice). Top them with a layer of sliced hard-boiled eggs.

Make a thick cheese sauce (see p. 64), adding a really good dollop of Dijon mustard to the mix (made-up English mustard may be added too, even German mustard if you have any), as well as plenty of pepper and salt.

Cover the egg layer with the mustardy, cheesy sauce, making sure that no egg or tomato shows through. Should you be using over-ripe, and thus rather liquid tomatoes, make the sauce even thicker, or don't use so many tomatoes. Sprinkle a little paprika over the surface and bake your dish in a medium oven, or slowly under the grill, until it is thoroughly heated through and smelling fine as it bubbles.

A more substantial dish may be made by adding very thin slices of meat, such as corned beef, cooked ham, or tongue, in between the tomato and egg layer. Leave gaps for the sauce to filter all the way down.

You can make this dish well in advance and then put it in the oven or under the grill ½ hour or more before it is wanted at the table. Always make sure that the pie is piping hot all through.

The Oldie Cookbook

This is important. Serve on its own or with a green salad.

YOU WILL NEED:

Tomatoes, fresh or canned
Hard-boiled eggs
Cheese sauce
Dijon mustard
Paprika
Very thinly sliced meat (optional)

Crispy Eggs and Toms

This crisper, sharper edition of the last recipe does without the sauce. It, too, may be made well before it is needed.

In a shallow, enamelled-iron or other fireproof dish, place a layer of sliced hard-boiled egg. Completely cover with a layer of sliced tomato (canned will do but omit the juice). Season well, squeeze over plenty of garlic, coat with toasted breadcrumbs and dribble over a goodish quantity of olive oil.

Place the dish under the grill to heat it through slowly, turning up the power to crispen the coating shortly before it is wanted at the table.

A little parsley sprinkled over the top looks good.

YOU WILL NEED:

Hard-boiled eggs
Tomatoes
Pepper and salt
Garlic
Toasted breadcrumbs
Olive oil
Parsley

142

Spanish Omelette

After a night spent in my home-made car/camper on a beach of
Spain's Mediterranean coast in the 1950s, where even the inquisi-
tive police had been beaten back by the vicious mosquitoes of that
time, I found a café open for a most welcome breakfast.

Would I like an omelette?

The lady owner slowly fried chopped onion and diced potato in
olive oil until they were cooked. Then she beat up a couple of
eggs with pepper and salt and poured them over the cooked
vegetables. One turn of the omelette and it was ready – a true and
delicious Spanish omelette. I have done the same many times
since.

YOU WILL NEED:

Onions
Potatoes
Olive oil
Eggs
Pepper
Salt

A Musseau

Many of us are inclined to use a vinaigrette only for salads involving vegetables. This is a pity. Any cooked meat such as pork, ham, lamb, beef or venison (either left over from a joint or bought ready cooked) given similar treatment is very appetizing.

Slice the meat thinly, arrange on a serving-dish and leave to marinate in a vinaigrette (see p. 67) to which you have added a mixture of some or all of the following: finely-chopped onion or shallot, capers, green peppercorns, chopped gherkins, pickled vegetables, pickled walnuts or chopped stoned olives. Just before serving, sprinkle over chopped parsley.

This is a delicious lunchtime dish with new or baked potatoes.

YOU WILL NEED:

Cooked meat
Vinaigrette
Onion or shallot
Capers
Green peppercorns
Gherkins or pickled vegetables
Pickled walnuts
Olives
Parsley

Cottage or Shepherd's Pie

This is an old favourite but few cookery books include the recipe. Shepherd's pie is made with minced lamb or mutton, cottage with minced beef. Leftovers are adequate, but minced, raw meat is by far the best. Have ready some stock, or stock cube dissolved in water, you will need about ½ pint per lb. of meat.

Fry chopped onion and, if desired, diced red or green pepper in dripping or other fat or oil. Cook until they are soft, then add the meat and fry for a little while longer.

Spice up your stock with tomato ketchup, pepper, salt, Worcestershire sauce and gravy browning. Add this to the meat then cover and cook slowly for 20–30 minutes.

Thicken the reduced cooking liquid with a little cornflour or potato flour mixed with cold water. Test for seasoning.

Put the mince into a pie dish (or other deep dish) or individual dishes and cover with a generous layer of mashed potato, made rather dry and without too much butter. Roughen up the surface with a fork.

Bake in a fairly hot oven until the pie is piping hot and the topping golden brown. If you make the pie in advance, reheat in a slower oven, turning it up towards the end.

You will need:

Minced meat
Dripping or oil
Onions
Red or green pepper (optional)
Stock
Tomato ketchup
Pepper and salt
Worcestershire sauce
Gravy browning
Cornflour or potato flour
Mashed potato

Shao Shao (or something like it)

In student days, this was one of the cheapest items on the menu at a Chinese restaurant in London's South Kensington. Just how it was made I do not know, but it was very easy to reproduce in 'digs' on a gas ring. This is how I still do it.

You will need the oriental 'five spices' with star aniseed as its most pungent ingredient. This is obtainable from oriental grocers and in most supermarkets.

Dice lean pork and fry in oil with some garlic. In a bowl mix a few good pinches of five spices, some soy sauce and ¼ crumbled stock cube. Add this to the pork and fry for a little longer. Now add enough water to come about half way up the meat. Cover the pan and cook until the pork is tender. Towards the end, when most of the liquid has evaporated, stir in a scant teaspoon of cornflour mixed with cold water. Cook for just a little longer to thicken the sauce. You probably won't need to add salt as the soy sauce and stock cube should have contributed enough.

Serve on a bed of hot noodles.

YOU WILL NEED:

Pork
Garlic
Oil
Five spices
Soy sauce
Stock cube
Cornflour
Noodles

Charcoaled Rissoles

The addition of lemon elevates these rissoles beyond the ordinary – even if conventionally fried or grilled. With that inimitable flavour of the barbecue they become quite irresistible.

Grind up uncooked lamb, mutton or beef with an unpeeled but de-pipped piece of lemon (or buy the meat minced and add finely chopped lemon). Into this mixture work some salt, milled pepper, a small beaten egg and some flour. It may seem a bit sloshy. Don't worry.

Mould into the desired shape and cook on the charcoal grill, turning once so that they become brown and crisp on both sides.

YOU WILL NEED:

Minced beef, lamb or mutton
Lemon
Pepper and salt
Egg
Flour

Irish Stew

Irish stew is a common enough dish. However, by adding any-thing other than the simple basic ingredients, it may be spoiled or become something that is not an Irish stew, although I have come across Irish cooks who insist on adding carrots. Perhaps there are no rules.

Slice plenty of onions and lay them thickly on the bottom of a cooking pot or pressure cooker. Add a layer of scrag end and middle (cheap lamb cuts from the neck end). Season well with pepper and salt. Top the meat with a thick layer of sliced potatoes. Pour in enough cold water to reach up to half the height of the ingredients.

Add no more, and do no more, other than pressure cook for 25–30 minutes or cover and cook gently on the top of the stove until the meat falls from the bone – about 1½ hours.

This classic dish is best made well in advance so that you can remove the layer of fat that solidifies above or around the pota-toes once it is cold. Re-heat the stew until it is piping hot before serving with a sprinkling of chopped parsley.

Note: For those, like children and oldies, who cannot cope or do not like dealing with bones, replace the traditional scrag end with minced lamb. Mix this with a little flour, pepper and salt and, if available, some freshly chopped mint. Roll into small balls and use instead of the cuts of lamb.

YOU WILL NEED:

Onions
Cheap (stewing) cuts of lamb
Potatoes
Pepper and salt
Chopped parsley

Black Pudding

Not very far from the Parisian *Académie Grande Chaumière* in Montparnasse, where the bosomy morning models posed nude and then touted for lunchtime trade, *boudin* (black pudding) was served to students at a most reasonable price in Wadja's Café. With bread and a carafe of red wine, it made a very satisfactory and economical meal. The dish can be made with a whole black pudding or with those made in a smaller sausage shape.

Gently fry 3–4 chopped onions in olive oil until they become transparent (but not brown). Add 4–5 chopped ripe tomatoes (or from a can). Season with pepper and salt then cover and cook gently for 10 minutes or so. Now take off the lid and continue cooking until the liquid reduces and the onion and tomato mix begins to thicken into a sauce. Pierce your black pudding in several places and place it in the sauce. Put the lid on the pan and cook very gently until it is hot right through.

Serve the black pudding covered in the sauce. How simple and cheap.

YOU WILL NEED:

Black pudding
Onions
Olive oil

Fresh or canned tomatoes
Pepper and salt

Bacon and Black and White Beans

Soak a 2–3 lb. piece of smoked bacon overnight in water. At the
same time soak half a packet of white haricot beans and the same
amount of black Chinese haricot beans.

The next day, pour a little water in your cooking pot or pressure
cooker, put in the bacon and surround with the soaked beans.
Add more water to cover the beans. Include a bay leaf and some
pepper and push 2 cleaned and scrubbed pig's trotters beneath
the surface of the liquid. Boil quickly for 10 minutes then cover
and cook slowly for around 2 hours or pressure cook for 30
minutes.

Extract the trotters (you could coat them in vinaigrette to eat as
a 'musseau', p. 144) and lift the bacon on to a serving dish.

Thicken the bean liquid with a little cornflour mixed with cold
water and cook for a while longer, stirring frequently. Test the
seasoning.

Slice the meat and serve covered with the beans and juices.

YOU WILL NEED:
A piece of smoked bacon
White haricot beans
Black Chinese haricot beans
Bay leaf
Pig's trotters
Pepper and possibly salt
Cornflour

Simple Cassoulet

This will not take long to make or cost a lot. It will warm and fill
those at your table on a cold winter evening.

Soak white haricot beans overnight. The next day, put them in a
saucepan or pressure cooker, cover well with stock and add a few

garlic cloves with small pieces of skin cut from pork chops that you will be adding later. Boil quickly for 10 minutes then cover the saucepan and simmer for around ¾ hour. Alternatively pressure cook for 20 minutes.

Pour off half the liquid from the pan (use in soup later), season the beans then throw in 1 pork chop per person (boned if desired), small pieces of smoked belly pork or bacon, and thick slices of Polish ring sausage. Simmer for 20–25 minutes until the chops are cooked or transfer to the oven and stew slowly for around an hour.

That's all. It really is so simple, and delicious with baked or mashed potatoes.

YOU WILL NEED:

White haricot beans
Stock
Garlic
Pepper and salt
Pork chops
Smoked belly pork or bacon
Polish ring sausage

'Will you still need me, will you still, feed me, when I'm 9½?'

Pop's Pasta

This simple pasta dish has always been a great favourite with my family. If there is any left over (seldom) it will be as good, if not better, when re-heated another day.

Cover the bottom of an oven-proof dish with a layer of meat sauce (see p. 65). Dribble over some olive oil and sprinkle with crushed garlic and oregano if desired.

Now boil fresh or dried pasta of any kind: spaghetti, macaroni, penne, noodles, lasagne, shells, spirals, etc., for 12 minutes (longer for the thicker shell-type pasta). Drain and spread this over the layer of meat sauce.

Next, and last, make a thinnish cheese sauce (white sauce with grated cheddar, see p. 64), adding a heaped teaspoon or more of Dijon mustard. Pour this over the pasta until no parts remain uncovered. Sprinkle some paprika over the surface if you like.

You can make this dish in advance, then all there is to do is bake it, uncovered, in a medium oven until the surface bubbles and begins to brown. Depending on your oven this could take 45 minutes to an hour or so. Be sure that it is piping hot all through as the top will tend to bubble before the inside is hot, especially if the dish has been allowed to cool down earlier.

You will need:

Meat sauce
Olive oil
Oregano or garlic (both optional)
Pasta of any kind (fresh or dried)
Cheese sauce, made with Dijon mustard
Paprika (optional)

Spaghetti with Rich Vegetarian Sauce

Fry 2–3 chopped onions and 1–2 crushed garlic cloves in plenty of olive oil. Throw in a chopped green pepper and fry for a little longer. Add a 14 oz. (400 g) can of chopped tomatoes and a handful of stoned and chopped olives (those with stones in have more flavour than those bought ready stoned). A little tomato purée will enhance the sauce no end. Add pepper and salt then simmer to reduce the liquid content.

Cook spaghetti for 12 minutes and serve with the sauce. Meat-eaters love this dish too.

YOU WILL NEED:

Onions
Garlic
Green pepper
Pepper and salt
Canned tomatoes
Tomato purée
Black olives
Dried spaghetti

153

Cabbage and Minced Beef

My Dutch wife, unused to cooking, announced that she would like to make a main course of cabbage and mince. The sound of this dish did not stimulate my salivary glands at all, but it turned out to be delicious, not to mention simple, quick and nourishing. This is how she makes it.

Heat olive oil in a large pan. Fry 1–2 chopped onions until they begin to brown. While the onion is cooking, work a beaten egg, a scant dessert spoon of curry powder, some toasted breadcrumbs, pepper and salt into 1 lb. or so of minced beef. Add this mixture to the browning onions and stir around over the heat until the meat changes colour.

Quarter and de-core a medium-sized, hard white cabbage, then slice it neither too coarsely or finely and boil in a little water until almost soft. Drain and add the cabbage to the cooked meat, stirring it all together. Serve with mashed potato.

Any left over may be mixed with mashed potato and baked in the oven or fried for another meal.

YOU WILL NEED:

Onions
Minced beef
Egg
Curry powder
Pepper and salt
Breadcrumbs
White cabbage

Free-standing Meat and Herb Pie

Buy, say, 1 lb. of minced pork and 1 lb. of minced veal or beef. Put these into a large bowl with the following ingredients: a good lump of fresh ginger, grated and fibreless, the flesh from 2 dozen black olives, 3 cloves of crushed garlic, salt, plenty of chopped fresh mint, coriander, or any herb of your choice, a very good milling of black pepper and the best part of 2 beaten eggs (reserve a little for later). Work this all together with a wooden spoon until an even blend has been obtained. Now stir in sifted flour to re-attain the original consistency that existed before adding the eggs.

Make some suet crust pastry (see p 161). Butter or oil a bread tin and roll out the dough so that there is enough to line the bread tin with plenty overhanging.

Fill the cavity with your mix. Fold the overhanging pastry over the top, trim as desired and seal together having first dampened the pieces that are to be joined. Decorate the surface with designs made from leftover bits, if you feel like it. Paint the remains of the beaten egg over the top of your pie to give it a nice colour when cooked. Make a vent hole for steam to escape by creating a chimney or piercing the pastry in several places. Bake the dish in a medium oven for 2–2½ hours.

'There's a little blue jacket in my rabbit pie, Mrs McGreggor!'

Serve hot by tipping it out of its tin on to a serving dish (not always easy). If to be served cold, dissolve some gelatine, with part of a stock cube if you like and, through the vent hole, fill the cavity within the pastry. Allow the pie to become cold before turning it out.

YOU WILL NEED:

Minced pork
Minced veal or beef
Fresh ginger root
Olives
Mint, coriander or other herb
Garlic
Eggs
Salt and milled pepper
Flour
Butter or oil
Suet crust pastry
Gelatine (optional)
Stock cube (optional)

Country Bean and Bacon Stew

This nutritious and delicious stew will feed masses and is simplicity itself to make. The combination of swede, beans and paprika is surprisingly successful, with the smoked bacon giving the dish a most inviting smell and taste. Needless to say, the soup made from any residue is a winner too.

Soak a quantity of dried beans (haricot, black-eye, red kidney, etc.) for several hours or overnight. Drain and throw them into a cooking pot or pressure cooker, with a few peeled cloves of garlic and plenty of diced swede. Half fill with water or stock and add salt, pepper and a lavish amount of paprika worked to a paste with a little water. On top place a single piece or several chunks of smoked, belly bacon with its skin on (best bought from a Polish delicatessen).

Boil vigorously for 10 minutes then simmer slowly for 1½–2 hours on the stove or in a low to medium oven. Alternatively, pressure cook for 25 minutes.

Just how much of each item and what kind of beans you use for this robust and filling dish is up to you.

YOU WILL NEED:
Dried beans
Garlic
Swede
Water or stock
Paprika
Pepper and salt
Smoked bacon

Skirt with Coriander Seeds

Buy a piece of trimmed, close-grained skirt (beef).

Break up a tablespoon to a handful of coriander seeds by roughly crushing them with the back of a wooden spoon in a bowl or in a pestle and mortar. Pound them into the beef with the flat side of a meat axe or rolling pin. The seeds may jump around a bit.

Make a vinaigrette with olive oil (see p. 67) adding a crushed garlic clove or two. Put the meat in a dish and cover with the vinaigrette. Turn the meat as often as you like for as long as you like. If you want to cook it a day or two later, put the dish in the refrigerator. (If the olive oil solidifies, allow it to warm up before turning the meat.)

Fry the skirt in its vinaigrette until both sides are well browned and the interior red.

Cut in the thinnest possible slices (across the grain). Serve with the juices and seeds. This dish is even better cold when it is easier to slice the meat thinly.

YOU WILL NEED:

Skirt of beef   Vinaigrette
Coriander seeds   Garlic

158

Puddings

I apologise for the paucity of recipes in this pudding section. The habit of those in my household, conscious that we already consume enough sugar in our diet without adding to it unduly, is to have an hors d'œuvre before the main course. Then, if anyone is still hungry, there may be cheese, fruit or ice-cream on offer.

However, sometimes the good fare of John Bull is demanded. So I start this section with the simple techniques of how to make pies and steamed puddings – both savoury and sweet. For, after all, it is such as these that have helped to form the character (and girth) of Britons over the ages.

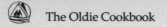

The Oldie Cookbook

Making Pastry

There are two simple kinds of pastry used for making tarts, pies and steamed puddings. They are **short crust** and **suet crust**. The first is for pies and tarts; the second for steamed puddings, sometimes for pies and tarts, dumplings in soups and stews, or for popping in around the joint as a kind of roast dumpling (when you might add English mustard in powder form to the dry mix).

Short crust pastry for pies is made by rubbing 2 oz. (50 g) of lard and 2 oz. (50 g) of butter into 8 oz. (225 g) of plain flour, i.e. **half the weight of fats to flour**, though these proportions may be altered a little. You can do it by eye quite successfully. The fats can be butter, lard, margarine, dripping or a mixture of your choice. Some add an egg yolk. There are no set rules. Then you will need a good pinch of salt, a little baking powder perhaps, and a little sugar if the pie is to be a sweet one. From this point, techniques tend to vary. Try cutting the fats into the flour with a couple of knives. Then rub the result between the fingers gently, allowing the crumbly pieces to fall back into the bowl from aloft. Now add cold water to make a firm dough. Roll it out on a floured board with a floured rolling pin before using it to line oiled dishes or to cover pies.

Pre-cook meats before adding them to pies. Always pierce vent holes in the pie crust for steam to escape. Support wide spans of pastry with an upturned egg cup or china piece made for the purpose.

Remember to dampen the edges of pastry that are to be joined together, and wet the pie-dish rim so that the pastry will adhere to it.

Paint milk or beaten egg over the surface of pastry to give the crust an appetizing look.

Pie fillings may be savoury: meat, game, fowl, rabbit, etc., all basking in their own thickened gravy: or sweet: fresh fruits such as blackberry and apple, or dried such as mincemeat, etc. When making an apple pie, boil up the skins, pips and cores with brown sugar and water. Mix the strained syrup with the apple to add to the flavour, or pour it over the surface of an open tart as a glaze. (See also p. 173.)

For **suet crust**, use half as much minced suet as self-raising flour, i.e. the same ratio of fat to flour as for short crust – it is easy to remember. Add salt to taste. Work the mixture between the fingers before adding just enough cold water to make a firm dough. Roll out as for short crust.

For steamed puddings, oil the basin and line it with roughly half the suet crust dough. Pour in the ingredients for a main course, such as cooked steak and kidney in gravy, sausage and onion, etc. Cover with a lid rolled out from the remaining dough, remembering to wet the edges so that they seal with the lining. For a sweet pudding, try golden syrup with grated or whole lemon, jam, marmalade or stewed fruits.

If the filling is fairly liquid, such as jam or golden syrup, alternate with layers of the rolled-out dough, again wet-sealed to the dough lining of the basin.

When complete, attach a clipped basin top or greaseproof paper (with centre pleat) held down by string or elastic. The traditional, and a very satisfying method, is to lay part of an old but clean sheet or pillow case over the top. Tie it around beneath the basin lip with string and knot the four corners together above.

Place a specially designed, perforated trivet, or upturned saucer (less satisfactory) in the bottom of a saucepan, upon which to rest the basin and which will protect the basin from bottom heat and from jumping around with the bubbles. Add cold water to the depth of an inch or two. Cover the saucepan, bring the water to the boil and allow the steaming to take place slowly for 2 to 3 hours. Check the water level occasionally and top up with boiling water as necessary. Steaming in a pressure cooker is much quicker, but follow the instructions for your make.

Steamed dishes like these seem to be out of favour. They shouldn't be. They are wonderful, especially in the winter.

YOU WILL NEED:
Flour
Fat
Egg (possibly)
Salt
Sugar for a sweet pastry
Savoury or sweet fillings

Hot Cake

A home-made cake, hot from the oven and served with chilled cream, ice cream, and/or a fruit purée or compote (perhaps laced with alcohol) makes a splendid pudding.

To make the cake is simplicity itself.

Take equal amounts in weight of butter, self-raising flour, eggs (2 weigh about 4 oz.) and a little less of sugar. Cream the butter and sugar, add the eggs, flour and a little baking powder. Beat it all together.

Add, perhaps, some raisins or sultanas the first time you make it. After that you could go on an adventure with one or more of the following: spices such as cinnamon, nutmeg, grated ginger, chopped preserved ginger; cocoa powder; morsels of marzipan; chopped nuts; chopped citrus fruit zest; sliced glacé cherries; chopped dried fruit such as figs, peaches, bananas, dates, pears and so on.

Turn the mixture into an oiled cake tin and cook in a moderate oven for 20–30 minutes. The time will depend on the depth of the cake and its position in the oven.

You will need:

Eggs
Butter
Flour
Sugar
Baking powder
Various additions

Flapjacks

These delicious, sticky morsels are simple to make and very handy for puddings, daytime snacks and children's tea parties. They are filling and irresistible.

Put a good lump of butter (up to 4 oz.) into a bowl. Open a can of golden syrup and put them both into a medium oven.

When the butter has melted and the syrup become less viscous, add 3 parts of syrup to the 1 part of butter in the bowl. Stir together and add porridge oats. Keep stirring in more oats until the result is a dryish, crumbly, sticky mess. At this stage it is optional to add sultanas and/or glacé cherries (they are really best plain).

Oil a large, shallow baking tin and tip the mixture in. Flatten it down with a dampened spoon and bake in a medium oven until the edges of the oat cake start to turn brown. This usually takes from 15 to 20 minutes. When cooked and while still hot, use a dampened knife or the end of a wide spatula to cut or push down through the cake and divide it into smallish squares.

When the flapjacks are quite cold, prise them out of their tin and break them into sections. Store them in a jar – they won't stay there long.

YOU WILL NEED:

Butter
Golden syrup
Porridge oats
Sultanas and/or glacé cherries (optional).

Raspberries and Blackcurrants

This simple and lovely recipe is ideal for those who freeze soft fruit from their garden or allotment. It is, of course, delicious when made with freshly-picked fruit.

Blackcurrants are a bit of a curse to pick cleanly, so rough-pick them straight into a saucepan (a few leaves and an insect or two won't matter). Simmer gently adding sugar to taste. When soft (about 10 minutes), squash well with a potato masher then strain off the juice through a sieve and throw away the pulp residue. Freeze the juice or pour it over fresh raspberries and serve with cream. If using from the frozen state take out both raspberries and blackcurrant juice 4 hours before they are wanted at the table.

YOU WILL NEED:

Blackcurrants
Raspberries
Cream

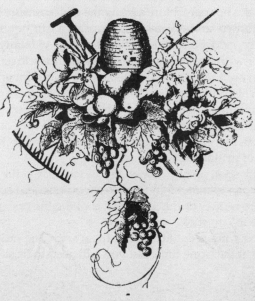

Versatile Thin Pancakes

These thin pancakes have always been a family favourite.

Put, say, 8 oz. of self-raising flour and a good pinch of salt in a bowl. Break an egg into a hole in the centre of the flour and, stirring and beating around from the centre outwards with a whisk, pour in a mixture of milk and water (half and half) until the batter is smooth and the consistency of single cream. Have the milk and water mix handy when you have finished, as the batter will slowly thicken and need thinning down.

Heat a frying pan on the stove. Make a thick wad of kitchen paper. Dip this into soft butter and rub it around the pan when it is quite hot so that the entire metal surface is coated very thinly. Tip in a spoonful of batter (you will soon discover the correct amount for your pan) and twist and rock it around until the bottom is covered with a thin coating.

When the edges start to shrink and go pale brown, turn the pancake over with a spatula. After a short time it will be cooked. Re-butter the hot pan before adding the next measure of mixture.

If not wanted immediately, the pancakes can be piled up in a warm place, or deep frozen, to be eaten later with any filling you like. Butter with jam or honey, and lemon juice with sugar are old favourites, but the choice is limited only by your imagination.

You can also cut them into sections and cover them or roll them up with savoury fillings to eat with drinks or to serve as an hors d'œuvre. Another excellent idea is to roll them around a savoury stuffing – fish, meat or vegetable – cover them with cheese sauce, and bake or grill them.

You will soon get to know the exact heat setting for your particular pan to make thin pancakes with ease and success.

Use more butter for the pan when cooking the first one. It is the only one liable to stick.

When you are adept at making them with one frying pan, try using two at the same time. But you will need to be sharp.

YOU WILL NEED:

Flour
Eggs
Salt
Milk
Butter

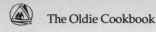

An Easy Café Liégeois

Take ordinary bulk vanilla ice-cream. Extract as much as you need from the container, allow to soften a little, then add Camp Coffee, or any other coffee essence, and stir until fully blended. Put into individual bowls and serve, covered with whipped cream if desired.

YOU WILL NEED:

Vanilla ice-cream
Camp Coffee (coffee essence)
Whipped cream

Ice-cream for Children

Children enjoy making their own ice-cream mixes – starting with a base of bulk-bought vanilla. Oldies can derive similar pleasure, perhaps employing one of the pricier, 'real cream' varieties as a base.

Camp coffee may be worked in (see the Café Liégeois recipe above) or poured over. Golden syrup or chocolate spread are two simple and fast 'sauces'. More glorious are golden syrup heated with butter, and the chocolate sauce recipe below. Jams, honey, chopped nuts, cereals, halva, and especially crumbled digestive or other biscuits, are all delicious additions.

For the more sophisticated palate you could stir in fruit purées or compotes, fresh or frozen, possibly laced with Cointreau or any other liqueur, sweet or dry.

YOU WILL NEED:

Vanilla ice-cream
The imagination of children, old and young

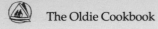

Chocolate Sauce for Ice-cream

This is an 'instant' winner with all chocolate lovers.

Melt butter in a saucepan. Stir in about twice its volume of white sugar. Add cocoa powder until the mixture becomes thick. Sprinkle in a few drops of vanilla essence.

Add water to attain the desired consistency.

Keep the mixture on the heat, whisking all the time, until it boils up to the rim of the pan. Allow to subside and repeat the operation.

Pour the sauce into a jug to serve hot or if preferred, leave to cool.

YOU WILL NEED:

Butter
Sugar
Cocoa powder
Vanilla essence

Ice-cream

Here are two recipes for those with ice-cream makers – especially suitable for the simple Donvier, or other 'frozen tub' machines.

Mango Ice-cream

Kulfi, the ice-cream of India, always tastes to me as if sweetened condensed milk is its main ingredient, so I tried mixing the contents of a 14 oz. (400 g) can of sweetened condensed milk with half the contents of a 30 oz. (850 g) can of mango pulp. The resultant ice-cream was an enormous success, and has been the house stand-by ever since.

YOU WILL NEED:

Sweetened condensed milk
Mango pulp

Very Chocolatey Rich Ice-cream

Put 3 heaped tablespoons of cocoa powder (Dutch cocoa seems to be the best) into a cooled bowl. Whisk in 10 fl. oz. of cooled single cream. Do not worry about a small lump or two of cocoa remaining in the mixture, these will turn into chocolate chips. Stir in 14 oz. (400 g can) of chilled sweetened condensed milk. Add the mixture to the tub and proceed in the usual way.

YOU WILL NEED:

Cocoa
Single cream
Sweetened condensed milk

The Oldie Cookbook

Nectarines in Aniseed

For those of us who are sometimes deceived by the state of nectarines on offer at market stalls and in shops, here is a fine way to make the best of the fruit when it is too ripe or where some parts of it are rotting while others remain quite hard.

Wash and dry the fruit, and cut inwards towards the stone to extract wedge-shaped pieces. Discard any rotten parts. Put the good pieces in a bowl and pour over a little ouzo (or other aniseed drink, such as Pernod or Ricard, etc.), then turn them over gently to coat all surfaces with the spirit.

Cover the bowl and keep it in the refrigerator until wanted. Turn the nectarines over every day if they are not to be eaten right away. Time will improve the taste. Serve with cream.

YOU WILL NEED:

Nectarines
Ouzo or another aniseed spirit

Tiny treacle puddings for people on diets.

Dad's Rustic Apple Pie

Wash, peel and core apples, of any kind. Put the peels, cores and pips into a saucepan with brown sugar and water to cover. Boil this mixture for quite a long time to extract all the good tastes. You may need to add more water.

Strain off the liquor (discard the solids) and return to the pan to reduce and thicken over the heat.

Cut up the flesh from the apples, place in a saucepan with white sugar and a little water and simmer to a pulp. Mash if desired or pass through a sieve or Mouli. Test for sugar content.

Make a pastry, either short crust or suet crust (see p. 160), or buy ready-made pastry if you can't stand the idea of making your own. Roll it out (fairly thinly) on to a floured surface and with it line an oiled tin or suitable pie-dish.

Put the unfilled pie in a medium oven to cook for 10 minutes or so. Then fill the pie with the apple pulp and decorate the surface with any patterns that your creative artistry will run to, using thin pieces of the leftover pastry.

Now pour the thickened liquid from the peels over the top – decorations as well – giving it a coating all over, and bake the pie in a medium oven until the pastry at the sides turns brown. Serve hot or cold (suet crust is better hot) with cream. This pie freezes well.

You will need:

Apples
White and brown sugar
Pastry (home-made or bought)

Gooseberries and Elder Flowers

One or two elder-flower heads added to gooseberries while they are stewing (in a little water with sugar) greatly enhances their flavour. Elders are to be found in both town and countryside (everywhere!) and they conveniently flower when gooseberries are ripe.

Extract the flower head before serving the gooseberries – simply with cream, in a pie, or whisked up into a fool with whipped cream or custard.

You will need:

Gooseberries
Elder-flower heads
Sugar
Water
Cream or custard, or both

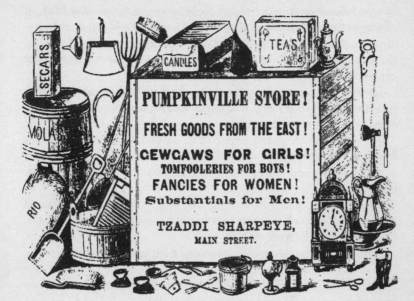

SECARS

MOLA

RIO

TEAS

CANDLES

PUMPKINVILLE STORE!

FRESH GOODS FROM THE EAST!

GEWGAWS FOR GIRLS!
TOMFOOLERIES FOR BOYS!
FANCIES FOR WOMEN!
Substantials for Men!

TZADDI SHARPEYE,
MAIN STREET.

Odds and Ends

In this chapter I have collected together recipes which somehow, because of their general nature, do not fit into the previous sections. They range from 'Mother of Vinegar' to 'No Need to Knead Bread' and include 'Yorkshire Pudding' and 'Pig's Head'. Many will ignore the two recipes that involve dealing with a pig's head. However, both dishes are most nourishing, delicious and very economical.

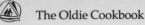

Tomato and Olive Base

I once returned from a holiday in Morocco with several kilos of olives to find that a large surplus of tomatoes had ripened in my absence. I stoned the olives, chopped up the tomatoes and cooked them together gently in olive oil with salt and pepper until most of the moisture had evaporated.

The resultant mixture was not only highly concentrated in taste, but also quite delicious. It can be served hot or cold with hot bread or toast, as an hors d'œuvre or with drinks.

It may be used to garnish or to stuff halved hard-boiled eggs for another decorative start to a meal.

It makes a good filling for omelettes, pancakes, vol-au–vents, canapés, etc.

Mixed with cooked rice and a raw egg, it becomes a splendid stuffing for any of the marrow family, as well as for peppers, tomatoes, onions, meat or fish.

Add a little to stews and casseroles, or liquidize to make a purée that could be used as a party dip; to flavour vinaigrette (or any other sauce or marinade); or even to 'paint' steaks, joints, fish or pieces of chicken, before roasting or grilling.

This versatile base also freezes splendidly.

YOU WILL NEED:

Tomatoes
Olives
Olive oil
Pepper and salt

Pickled Olives and Apricots

This concoction, because of its colourful, spicy and palate-cleansing nature, makes a fine, festive assortment from which to pick at with drinks. It also serves well as a pickle to counter rich or fatty food.

Take a quantity of dried apricots and cover them with boiling water for a short time to wash off preservatives and noxious matter. Drain and place them in an enamelled saucepan. Cover with good wine or cider vinegar adding the following spices: a pinch of blade mace, 4–5 cardamoms, half a dozen cloves and the same number of juniper berries. Bring slowly to the boil and simmer for a few minutes until the liquid has *almost* disappeared. Then leave the mixture to get cold. The apricots will have absorbed the spiced vinegar but will remain quite firm in texture.

Take a good-sized jar (that can be well sealed), and half-fill with the apricots, spices and any remaining juices. Mix in black Kalamata olives, well drained of their brine, and some good olive oil. Pack the jar fairly tightly. Put on the lid and turn the jar upside down until the olives and apricots are well coated with the liquid. Do this every so often to keep the contents moist and happy. The mixture will keep for months and months.

Serve in a white bowl for guests to pick at when drinking, or as a pickle to complement pork or other rich food.

Made in late November, you will have a most interesting treat in store for Christmas and beyond.

YOU WILL NEED:
Dried apricots
Vinegar (wine or cider)
Black olives
Olive oil
Blade mace
Cloves
Cardamoms
Juniper berries

No Need to Knead Bread

Because this recipe is so long, you may think that to make bread by my method will be tedious and time-consuming. I can assure you that when you get the hang of it, nothing could be easier, or more rewarding. You will make the mixture in 5–10 minutes, ignore it as it rises, and return later to bake it for 1 hour.

The overall time involved in creating this easy-to-make, no-need-to- knead bread will depend on the degree of warmth at the 'rising'. It may take from 2 to more than 4 hours from start to finish, depending on circumstances. Here is the recipe:

Take a 3 lb. (1.5 kg) packet of bread-making flour – wholemeal flour is excellent but rises slowly, rye flour gives most taste but is the least inclined to rise, white rises the quickest. A mixture of ⅛ packet or less of rye flour to 1 packet of white bread flour is, I think, one of the better combinations. Add a tablespoon of dried yeast and a tablespoon of salt. Give it a good stir. (The ingredients should be warm, especially in the winter.)

Slowly pour in about 3 pints of hot, but not boiling water, stirring all the time. (The amount of water varies according to the source and type of flour.) You can dissolve in the water a level teaspoon of black molasses, golden syrup, honey (I use it), sugar or maple syrup to help the yeast multiply and do its job.

The mixture should be gooey and slightly elastic – a sort of thick, sticky porridge – one that will just pour out of the bowl when helped with a wooden spoon. If the mixture is sloppy, it may overflow from the bread-tin as it rises. (The wetter the mixture the more moist will be the interior of the bread.) At this point, you can also add one or more of the following: nuts, dates (or other dried fruit), bananas, marzipan, olives – all chopped – or any other ingredient that might take your fancy, remembering that the more bits and pieces you add, the slower it will rise. It is better to start with and succeed in making plain bread. Experiment later.

Very generously butter 3 large bread tins, or 2 large and 2 small ones. Leave small lumps of butter or margarine adhering to the inside of the tins. Dust this fatty surface with flour, or if you want

to create a rustic look to your loaves, use porridge oats instead -
these will also make it easier to extract the loaves when cooked.
Now ease the bread dough into the greased tins, filling them no
more than half to two-thirds full. An uneven surface will not
matter. Place them, with a gap between each, on a tray to rise in a
warm place away from draught (the tray will catch any mixture if
the tins overflow). Good places are near a hot stove or boiler.
There is no need to cover the tins. The time it will take for the
volume to increase by the optimum amount (to about the top of
the tin) will depend on the degree of warmth around the tins.
Expect at least 3 hours but don't leave overnight.

When you think the mixture has risen enough, slide the tins
gently into a very hot oven. Don't shake or bang them en route.
Give them half an hour at this high setting. Then turn down the
heat to give them another 30 minutes (slightly less for smaller

loaves) at a medium setting. The smell of baking bread will be wonderful.

When the hour is up, tip the loaves out of their tins and allow them to cool on a wire-mesh rack. Once they are completely cold you can freeze any surplus loaves (they will be in perfect condition when unfrozen again). Alternatively, home-made bread makes a fine gift for friends. Since the interior is more moist than 'bought' loaves, they will keep fresh for very much longer, and you can prevent the crust from hardening by placing a polythene bag over the top (or by storing the bread in a bag in the refrigerator).

Could real, yeasted bread be easier or more economical to make? Of course there is a snag. The residual dough mixture will stick to the mixing bowl and spoon in a most tenacious way, and be the very devil to wash up.

YOU WILL NEED:
Flour
Yeast
Salt
Butter or another fat
Rolled oats

A Treat to Enjoy with Drinks

Margaret Costa, the well known cookery writer, came to visit one day. I made a gougère. It did not turn out as it was supposed to, but our culinary guest loved the result. There must, I thought, be an easier and quicker way of reproducing such a delicious failure. The following is the result of my experiments, and it is excellent when eaten with drinks.

Put about ½ lb. of self-raising flour into a large bowl with some pepper and salt. Break an egg or two into a depression in the centre and add a good dollop of Dijon mustard. Whisk the eggs and, as you do so, take in flour from the periphery. Add milk, whisking and beating all the time, until the mixture is smooth yet thick. Grate in, say, 6 oz. of cheddar cheese (too much may make the treat oily). Stir again.

Oil a frying-pan generously and fry some chopped garlic until it turns brown. Now pour in the mixture (enough to form a ¼-inch thick 'pancake'), cover the pan and cook gently. When the surface of the pancake begins to form a skin and show signs of bubbles, it is time to toss it, or turn it over as best you can. With its brown side uppermost, cut slits in the top to allow moisture to escape from within. Continue cooking uncovered, and after 5–10 minutes lift a corner to inspect the under side. When cooked and brown, turn the pancake on to a board and cut it into manageable pieces or present it whole with a knife so that your guests can cut off their own slices.

YOU WILL NEED:
Self-raising flour
Salt and pepper
Eggs
Dijon mustard
Milk
Cheddar cheese
Oil
Garlic

The Oldie Cookbook

Two Lemony Stuffings

These two lemony stuffings add zest to meats.

Fry 3–4 chopped onions and about ½ lb. chopped mushrooms in some dripping, butter or oil until soft. In a bowl, crumble 7–8 slices of soft bread, breaking it up with your fingers into smallish crumbs. Add the onion and mushroom, and plenty of finely-cut fresh sage, or crumbled, dried sage. Coarsely grate in the rind of a scrubbed lemon. Season with pepper and salt, then add a beaten egg. Stir it all together and that is stuffing number one.

Boil some rice (brown is better) until soft. Strain it well and put it into a bowl with the grated peel of a scrubbed lemon and just a little of the juice. Add pepper and salt and a beaten egg and stir it all together.

The stuffing is rather sloppy at this stage, but will firm up well when cooked.

YOU WILL NEED:

FIRST STUFFING
Onions
Mushrooms
Dripping, butter or oil
Breadcrumbs
Sage
Pepper and salt
Lemon
Egg

SECOND STUFFING
Rice
Lemon
Pepper and salt
Egg

Two Turkey Stuffings

Combine sausage meat with half its volume of freshly rubbed breadcrumbs. Add pepper, salt and dried thyme and transfer to a saucepan. Cook over a moderate heat stirring all the while. Allow to cool before using.

Rub enough breadcrumbs to make a little under the volume of stuffing you require. Add plenty of finely-diced onion, cooked to the transparent stage in olive oil, and an equal quantity of cooked, peeled and chopped chestnuts (slit them across the apex before boiling). Mix these together with a handful of finely-cut fresh sage (or finely-rubbed if dried). Bind with an egg or two, depending on the volume, and season with pepper and salt.

YOU WILL NEED:

FIRST STUFFING

Sausage meat
Fresh breadcrumbs
Pepper and salt
Thyme

SECOND STUFFING

Breadcrumbs
Onion
Olive oil
Sage
Chestnuts
Egg
Pepper and salt

Jon. Cramer.

Yorkshire Pudding

My Yorkshire puddings had never been a success until a neighbour, a Yorkshireman whose only forays into the kitchen had been to make his native delicacy, told me his recipe. I have kept more or less to it ever since and have not had a failure. Here are his secrets.

Put dripping or cooking oil into a large baking tin and put the tin in a hot oven, then make your mix.

Have ready ½ pint of liquid: 3 parts water to 1 part milk. Then sieve 7 heaped dessertspoons of plain flour into a bowl. Add a good pinch of salt. Break 3 small or 2 large eggs into a hole in the centre of the flour. With a whisk, gradually take in the flour from the centre outwards adding the liquid slowly as you go. When all the liquid has been incorporated beat the batter with the whisk to make sure there are no lumps remaining.

Take the very hot pan from the oven, ensure the sides and bottom are coated with fat, then add the batter which should immediately start to curl up at the edges.

Return the pan to the hot oven for, give or take, 30 minutes.

YOU WILL NEED:

Dripping or cooking oil
Plain flour
Salt
Milk and water
Eggs

Versatile Pulses

Pulses, such as chick peas, soya beans, red beans, black-eye beans, lentils, peas, broad beans, navy beans, lima, haricot, flageolets, butter beans etc., in their freshly podded or dried state, are full of nourishment, minerals, vitamins and roughage – inexpensive, too. But beware of the air they can produce in the stomach and tubes further along!

All dried beans should first be soaked in plenty of cold water. Beans without their skins, and small beans, should be soaked overnight, or for 12 hours. Large beans in skins, such as broad (fava) and butter beans, need 24 hours (change the water after 12 hours to prevent them from fermenting). All will swell and absorb quite a bit of liquid.

Once they have been soaked, **all dried beans should first be boiled fast for 10 minutes.** These instructions have resulted from the discovery that red kidney beans, cooked below boiling point in slow cookers, became toxic. So when slow cooking, by whatever method, be sure to boil beans for 10 minutes before lowering the heat.

Dried peas need to be cooked for about half an hour, small beans and lentils much the same, broad beans and other large beans for up to 2 hours. All should be simmered very gently. Make sure that beans are well cooked before you eat them.

Most of these beans can be boiled and served cold as an hors d'œuvre when mixed with some salad oil, chopped onion, and then sprinkled with chopped parsley or other herb. They can be combined with any number of ingredients including canned fish, such as sardines, anchovies and tuna; meat, such as chopped ham, bacon, chicken, etc.; chopped vegetables, olives, gherkins, and so on.

You can serve them as a hot or cold vegetable, plain or in a creamy or spicy sauce.

Now let's make a stew-type bean dish with, say, soya beans: Fry some chopped onion and garlic in olive or other oil. Add small pieces of belly of pork and chopped mushrooms. When these have browned, transfer them to a fireproof pot and add the beans (pre-soaked and drained), some pepper and salt (some people add salt at the end) and perhaps a herb. Cover with water or stock, put the lid on the pan and boil quickly for 10 minutes then cook very slowly on the top of a stove, or in a low oven until the beans are tender (see rough times above). Top up with water as necessary during cooking to prevent the dish from drying out .

Try the same with another pulse, such as lentils, but this time add some tomato purée or a can of tomatoes. Omit the meat if you like.

To make a substantial main course with red beans (soaked overnight): Fry chopped onion and garlic. Add the beans and water and fast boil for 10 minutes. Now add pieces of fatty, smoked bacon and chunks of potato and simmer until the ingredients are tender and most of the liquid absorbed.

Having enjoyed beans as an hors d'œuvre, a vegetable, or a main course, turn any left over into soup by just adding water or stock. You may well want to jazz up the taste a bit, so it is worth remembering that tomato ketchup contains sugar, vinegar and tomato – splendid ingredients for improving soups or stews. Worcestershire sauce also enhances flavour, so does a pinch of curry powder. A dash of vinegar with a pinch of sugar always helps soups like these.

Should you feel like it, half an hour before the bean dish or soup is ready, add some broken-up noodles, penne, or other dried pasta. Pulses and pasta combine well.

Note: Broad (fava) beans are very easy to grow. You can eat them whole when the pods are very small (the flavour is very strong at this time). Leave some pods to dry and blacken on the stem. Then harvest them to dry out further in a greenhouse or other warm spot. Then pod them and keep them in a warm place until they rattle when disturbed. Save some of these dried beans for next year's seed. Store the rest in a jar for winter feasts, or use as counters for children's games.

You will need:
Dried pulses of your choice, and imagination

Eggs

Boiled, Scrambled, Devilled, Omeletted and on the Plate

For the perfect boiled egg, place at room temperature in a pan reserved for eggs alone. Cover with cold water and bring to the boil. At the exact moment of boil, time for 2½ minutes for large eggs, 2¼ for medium and 2 for small. Extract from the boiling water and eat immediately – preferably with buttered 'fingers' of toast for dipping into the yolk.

For scrambled eggs, melt some butter in a saucepan. Add a little oil and pepper and salt. Break in the required quantity of eggs and slowly and continually stir them from the sides of the pan inwards with a wooden spoon. Serve them just before they are cooked through and they will be perfect.

To devil them, add some Dijon mustard and a few capers after you have broken the eggs into the pan. Continue as for scrambling.

For an omelette, use 2 eggs at a time. Break them into a bowl and add pepper and salt. At this stage, you may like to add finely-chopped chives, parsley or both. Roughly beat the eggs. Now melt a good lump of butter in your frying pan or omelette pan and shake it around until the cooking surface is quite coated. Tip the excess butter into the egg mix, beat together and tip into the hot pan. Now slowly draw in the cooked egg from the circumference to the middle, tipping the pan to allow uncooked egg to take its place. Just before the omelette is cooked (it won't take long) fold it over and slide on to a warmed plate. Repeat the operation as necessary.

For a sorrel omelette, take half a dozen or so sorrel leaves. Tear the greenery from the central 'spines' and throw away these fibrous parts. Heat some oil and butter in your frying or omelette pan, add pepper and salt and cast in your leaves. Stir them around gently until they soften and change to an olive-green colour. Beat 2 eggs in a bowl, stir in the sorrel and oils then return this mixture to the pan and cook as above. This is a wonderful dish.

An 'egg on the plate' is cooked, and then eaten, on a flat or shallow fireproof dish with handles – the heavier the better. Heat some olive oil on it then break in an egg or two. Cover the dish with a lid and cook the eggs until the yolk is no longer transparent and the edges of the white have begun to turn brown. Add salt and pepper and serve them in the dish with bread or toast to dip into the tasty liquids.

You will need:

Eggs
Ingredients according to the recipes

Cheesy Matters

People buy cheese covered with ground pepper, or blended with garlic and herbs, yet it is so easy to make at home. Milk, turned sour naturally or with rennet, if poured into a muslin-lined basin, then tied and hung up to drain, makes the basis for many an excellent home-made, peppered or herbed cheese.

You can enliven a (bought) plain cream or curd cheese by rolling it in freshly-milled pepper, chopped herbs or spicy seeds such as poppy or crushed coriander. Alternatively, these ingredients can be worked in with olive oil and possibly garlic.

Individual soft cheeses such as goat's or sheep's can be enhanced by marinating for a while in olive oil – plain or mixed with chopped herbs. More simply, milled black pepper or chopped herbs sprinkled over the top adds greatly to both looks and flavour.

Besides bread and biscuits, what goes well with cheese? Fruit, especially apples and fresh figs, go handsomely with cheese, as does the countryman's traditional accompaniment of raw onion. Cheese and olives make a fine marriage. However, supremely good is the combination of cheese and a plain lettuce salad – made with the simple dressing of oil, vinegar, pepper and salt.

YOU WILL NEED:
Cheese
Your chosen accompaniments

Mayonnaise Toast

You have made your mayonnaise (see p. 68) and found some left over after a meal.

For breakfast the following morning, or for a child's light tea, put the mayonnaise into a shallow dish or plate, add pepper and salt, and whisk in some milk.

Allow this liquid to soak into slices of bread then fry them until both sides are golden brown.

You will need:

Mayonnaise
Pepper and salt
Milk
Slices of bread

'Arnold's just had his memoirs confiscated by Scotland Yard's Obscene Publications Department'

BLT

Escaping from the austerity of wartime England to learn to fly in Oklahoma, it was almost a miracle to see and be offered so much food to eat. But after a while, a diet that included salad cream on fruit salad and its like, I craved for something that was not cooked in bulk for service personnel. BLT was the answer. This is still, to my mind, one of America's greatest culinary inventions. The different temperatures and contrasting tastes and textures of bacon, lettuce and tomato make it an absolute winner – and it is so simple to make.

Toast two slices of bread. Fry thin slices of streaky bacon until crisp and almost fat-free. Dry off any excess fat with kitchen paper. Slice some tomato. Wash and dry some crisp lettuce.

Spread mayonnaise on a slice of toast. Place on it a layer of bacon, lettuce and tomato. Dust with pepper and salt. Spread the other slice of toast with the mayonnaise and, with mayonnaise side down, place it on top to complete the sandwich.

YOU WILL NEED:
Toast
Mayonnaise
Streaky bacon
Lettuce
Tomato
Pepper and salt

Tartar Buns

Of the many foods I look forward to when visiting Holland, raw herrings, smoked eel, stroopwafels, Brokkel Oude cheese, and these raw beef buns (broodje tartaar) are favourites.

Buy finest minced beef fillet (you won't need much) and mix with chopped shallot or onion and capers (dried in kitchen paper first). Season with salt and pepper. That's it. Fill bread buns or baps with this raw beef mixture – a simple and wonderful picnic treat for those who like raw beef.

YOU WILL NEED:

Minced beef fillet of the finest quality
Shallots or onion
Capers
Salt and milled black pepper
Soft bread buns or baps

Bacon matters

One of the most useful additions to your larder is very thinly sliced, smoked, streaky bacon.

It is obtainable in supermarkets, but far better to seek out one of the last remaining traditional grocers (the sort of shop where the smell of freshly ground coffee mingles deliciously with that of smoked hams and cheeses) who will skin and very thinly slice a gristle-free piece. (It is an even greater advantage if he will shrink-wrap the cut slices in small amounts.) These, or the supermarket packets, may then be deep-frozen and used when wanted. They will not take long to unfreeze. The bacon will keep for ages in the freezer and a long time in the refrigerator if unopened. You will then have a constant supply – obtainable with the minimum of fuss and trouble. It is economical, too.

This bacon has a multitude of uses, mainly after it has been crisply fried and de-fatted with kitchen paper. Some examples of the wide variety of ways in which it can be used are as follows:

In sandwiches (BLTs in particular) and other fillings or stuffings (for avocados, pancakes, poultry, etc.).

In salads (particularly good with raw spinach, rocket or sorrel).

With terrines, liver and game.

With vegetables, such as Brussels sprouts (see p. 79), broad beans (see p. 29), cabbage, leeks, tomatoes, and with mushrooms.

In pasta dishes.

With pulses such as haricots, lentils, split peas, etc.

In stews and casseroles, savoury pies and tarts.

With egg.

Streaky bacon has the advantages of being nearly fat-free, concentrated in taste, and crisp in texture after being fried for a short time.

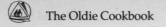

Bacony Eggs

This simple dish may be eaten hot or cold.

Use kitchen scissors to cut rashers of thinly-sliced, rindless streaky bacon into small pieces. Fry until crisp. Then herd them to the side of the frying pan so that you can pour off the surplus fat and then dab the residue with kitchen paper. Be careful not to burn yourself when doing this. Add a little olive oil, pepper, salt (if the bacon is not too salty) and 2 eggs for each person. Stir the bacon and eggs together and cook until the eggs are very nearly done. Slide the mixture on to a hot serving dish.

Sprinkle chopped parsley over the top if it is to be served hot. Add a little olive oil and a sprinkling of paprika or chilli-con-carne powder if it is to be served cold.

YOU WILL NEED:

Bacon
Olive oil
Pepper and salt
Eggs
Parsley, paprika or chilli-con-carne

Coffee

For those who enjoy real coffee and would like to make it at the speed of the 'instant' product, try this.

Find a coffee shop where your favourite roasted beans can be ground to the finest powder – known as 'pulverized' or 'Turkish ground'. Use it as you would 'instant'. A heaped teaspoon is generally enough for one cup. Give the coffee a good stir after pouring in the boiling water.

The main advantage is that you will always be able to drink 'real' coffee without the normal hassle involved. The disadvantage is that there will be grounds at the bottom of the cup.

Store the powder in an air-tight, glass jar and keep this in the refrigerator to extend the coffee's 'fresh' life.

YOU WILL NEED:

Pulverized or Turkish ground coffee

The Oldie Cookbook

Horseradish

Horseradish is underrated as a flavouring and as a sauce. I believe this to be because the root, being very strong and tasty in its original form, is 'bulked up' for commercial sauces with such as turnip – and ends up as an uninviting shadow of its true, powerful and flavoursome self.

In order to obtain the real, biting, eye-watering, pungent original, make the concentrate yourself, and store until wanted.

First find your horseradish. One of the best sources happens to be allotments. The nature of this root is to 'take over' land and become difficult to eradicate, so allotment holders are often more than pleased for you to help them extract the pernicious plant from their plots or to tell you where they grow.

Medium-sized roots are best. The largest are inclined to be woody. Scrub the roots well (it is not really necessary to peel them), cut into smallish pieces and put them into a blender with some salt, vinegar and a little plain yoghurt. If using a pestle and mortar, cut the roots up as finely as possible beforehand, and be prepared to cry. Obtain a rough, dryish purée, and put this into air-tight jars. Store the jars in the refrigerator.

You can add cream or yoghurt to modify and soften the horseradish 'bite' when making your blend for the table. But it is best used when not too diluted – for roast beef, smoked fish such as trout or mackerel, stuffing (eggs especially) and flavouring.

You will need:
Horseradish roots
Salt
Vinegar
Yoghurt

196

Pig's Head

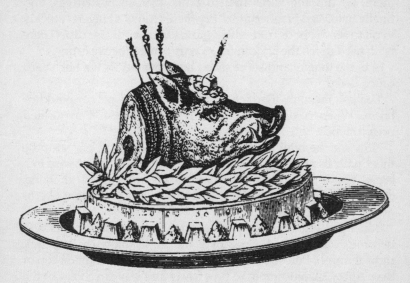

Refrain from reading this if you do not like the idea of dealing with a pig's head, but if you like eating this kind of food, or if you are short of cash and hungry, read on.

Get a butcher to divide a pig's head for you (he'll remove the eyes), or buy half a head. Select one that has been well de-bristled.

Extract the brain and cover it for a short time with boiling salted water. Remove the outer membrane. Fry slices of the brain in butter, to which you have added a little vinegar and a few capers.

Cut off the ears. Wash the head and ears thoroughly, and put them in well-salted water for 12 hours or more. Then boil in a very large pot with bay leaves, peppercorns, garlic, onion, carrots, celery and the like. When the meat will fall from the bone (this takes hours) lift out both head and ears, and when cool take the meat off the bone. Use the juices and vegetables as the basis for soup or, strained, for stock.

Tackle the cooked ears, which have a certain crunchiness to them, by dipping slices first in flour, then in beaten egg and finally in toasted breadcrumbs. Fry these (Angel's Fingers) quickly in oil to serve hot or cold with a garlicky, mayonnaise dip. (There is no need to tell the squeamish **exactly** what they are eating.)

Skin the tongue and serve sliced and covered with a hot, sharp sauce (see p. 67)

The jaw meat, or 'Bath chap', can be pressed into a mould or basin. When cold, take it from the bowl and roll in toasted breadcrumbs. Slice for the table.

Now for the brawn, to be made from all that is left: slice the meat with its skin into thinnish strips. Lay these lengthwise in a bread tin or like container, interspersed with sliced gherkins, chopped onion, garlic, parsley, or anything else you might like, to give it a 'house' style.

Boil up a little of the cooking liquid so that it reduces and becomes concentrated. Pour over the meat, allowing it to sink right through. Put a board or plate on top and a weight on top of that. Allow surplus liquid to flow away and leave to cool. Cut the brawn in slices in its pot, or heat the container under hot water and turn the brawn out on to a serving dish. Eat brawn slices with hot potatoes and salad, or in sandwiches. Serve with mustard.

From such a modest outlay you have obtained: a small dish of brains; ample stock; boiled vegetables in a soup; ears mayonnaise; tongue with a sharp sauce; Bath chap; brawn galore. It's unbelievable!

YOU WILL NEED:

A half or whole pig's head
Salt
Butter, vinegar and capers for the brains
Vegetables and spices for the boiling
Flour, egg, breadcrumbs and garlic mayonnaise for the ears
Sharp sauce for the tongue
Gherkins, herbs, onion, etc., for the brawn

Hot Head

This rough and hearty country dish will warm the vitals on a winter's day.

Take half a pig's head, clean it, brine it, and pare away the meat from the bones (you will need a very sharp, pointed knife). Put the meat through a coarse mincer, omitting the snout, ear, eye and brain, then place in a bowl with capers, vinegar, green peppercorns, pepper, salt, some flour and an egg. Beat all this together, then put it into a bread tin and bake in a slow to moderate oven for 2 hours or until the edges and top are crispy brown.

Drain off any liquid and dish out the hot meat. Serve with chunks of hot bread.

Turn the bones, snout and ear into stock. And if you extract the cooked ear from the stock, it will be excellent to eat, hot or cold, with a sauce (see p. 198).

YOU WILL NEED:
Half a pig's head
Capers
Vinegar
Green peppercorns
Pepper and salt
Flour
Egg

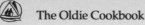

Yorks with everything

If you have meat roasting in the oven with space around it, make a Yorkshire pudding batter (page 184) and, about half an hour before the meat is ready, pour off excess fat into your dripping-pot, surround the meat with batter, turn up the oven and carry on with the cooking. Check the Yorkshire. Thicker batter may take longer.

Suppose you are roasting a chicken. Before you put the bird into the oven, cut up onions and peeled potatoes and put them round the chicken in the roasting tin. Coat the vegetables with melted dripping or oil before putting them in the oven with the chicken and pour batter over them at the correct time.

Adding batter is a possibility whenever you cook meat or vegetables in the oven.

YOU WILL NEED:

Yorkshire pudding batter

Mother of Vinegar

One way or another I have had tremendous fun and satisfaction
from my various mothers of vinegar. They have provided me for
years with the finest vinegar at very little cost.

Buy a vinegar jar (*vinaigrier* in France), or two if you want to
make both wine and cider vinegar. These are of glazed, brown
stoneware, bulbous in shape, lidded, and have a wooden tap set
in a corked collar about a third of the way up.

Pour in dry red, white or rosé wine (or mixed) in which you can
find no trace of sulphur. Add enough to adequately cover the tap
outlet. Replace the lid and wait, hopefully, until a mother has
been created. Initially she will be thin, and look like an opaque
disc of reddish jelly – probably resting on the top of the liquid, or
just under it. This creation may take months. If you add a piece
from an existing mother in another jar it will speed up the process
no end. A good degree of surrounding warmth will also help.
Don't be afraid to put your hand and arm inside the jar to feel if
she has arrived.

With a mother in situ, she must be fed with wine or wine dregs
regularly. Try not to neglect her for more than two or three weeks
or she will starve. Wine tipped in to keep her upper surface moist
is essential.

Once the vinegar has become strong enough, you may draw it
off when wanted, making sure that the contents of the jar are
always above tap level.

Use this delicious, tangy vinegar with caution. It will usually be
far stronger than that obtainable from the shops.

A wine vinegar mother will help to create cider vinegar – and
vice versa, but cider and wine vinegar manufacture should be
kept separate.

For pickling, cider vinegar is the cheaper to make. Almost fill
the jar (they usually hold about 5 litres) and when the cider has
reached the required vinegar strength, pour it into screw-top
glass bottles. If you like, sterilize the vinegar by placing the
uncapped bottles in a bain-marie for 20 minutes at 160F (71C).
Screw on the bottle tops when hot.

Alcohol is necessary for the manufacture of vinegar, so non-alcoholic wine or American sweet cider will not do at all. Once the process is under way, ignore what goes on inside your jar. Several mothers and children will form inside, any of which you may spare for a friend about to enter upon this delightful aspect of culinary husbandry.

After a year or so, delve in and discard tired and ancient mothers who will, by then, be taking up too much room and may even start to block the tap.

All this may sound a little 'earthy', but for most of the time you will just see a handsome jar in the kitchen, and be able to use the finest vinegar obtainable – almost for free. You will also have a good use for wine dregs.

Dripping

Animal fats may be out of fashion for those with health or slimming problems. Nevertheless, a balance in food as in nature is absolutely necessary.

Good dripping adds wonderful flavours to a roast (especially to roast potatoes) as well as to numerous other dishes.

The three best constituents of a dripping blend are: dripping obtained from the roasting of a duck or goose, lard (bought in a block), and the dripping from a beef-roasting – preferably a forerib joint. Thereafter, any other 'drippings' may be incorporated. You can amalgamate them all by putting your dripping-pot in a hottish oven (when you've turned it off after cooking a roast, for example). Refrigerate when cold.

When making a stew, gravy, soup or stock, cut out the solid dripping from above and put it aside. Use the wonderful brown jelly that lies beneath to enhance both colour and flavour – far better than stock cubes. This jelly is one of the great bonuses of dripping-pot culture.

Bread or toast spread with dripping is one of the lost delights of this health-conscious world. Spread, then sprinkle a little salt over and mill some pepper on top, then guzzle. I once gave this delicacy to some gourmet visitors from Belgium, calling it *Pâté Anglais*. They raved about it.

Stock and the Fun of Making It

You will always need stock. The easy way is to dissolve a stock cube in boiling water or in the liquid of your dish. A small amount of instant, concentrated stock will be found in jellified form at the bottom of your dripping pot (see previous page). To make stock yourself requires more time but little effort, and the result freezes very well.

You can boil up bones, hooves, trotters (excellent) and the odd chicken or other carcass to make a stock. A more variable, on-going sort of stock can be made according to the following 'continuous' method:

You can use a saucepan, pressure cooker (the quickest way), or if you have an Aga (or similar cooker) an oven-proof pot. This method usually starts with a roast chicken carcass or bone of roast meat, left-over bones and the solidified jelly and bits remaining in the pan. If you have made gravy with these bits and pieces, then add whatever remains in the gravy jug. Put these ingredients into your chosen cooking vessel with enough water to cover. Then add pepper and salt, a bay leaf or two, herbs (but be careful not to overwhelm the stock with the taste of a distinctive herb), a small pinch of blade mace perhaps, some peppercorns, coriander seeds, a couple of cardamom seeds, a clove or two, some turmeric if you want to colour it yellow, a small piece of a cinnamon stick, and on it goes.

Bring up to the boil and either simmer slowly for 2–3 hours (with the lid on), or pressure cook for, say 35 minutes, or leave in the slowest oven of the Aga for anything from 6 to 24 hours. Once this base is made you can keep using and adding to it as described in the following paragraphs.

You can use your stock for boiling pasta, or rice, or for cooking vegetables such as cabbage, carrots, leeks, potatoes, asparagus, etc. When the cooking is finished, return the water to the stock pot. Its viscosity will have been altered, and become tastier in the process.

Skins of vegetables may be added as you peel or cut them. You might add the outer leaves of cauliflowers or cabbages, the woody stems of asparagus, the outer layers of onions, the residue from squashed garlic, leek tops, onion tops, etc. Boil them up as above.

Eventually, the bones and other ingredients will relinquish their flavours. Throw them away and start again.

You may find this stock has taken on the form of an excellent soup before you've really noticed it. If you want to give this 'body', add a few chopped vegetables, some cooked beans and perhaps some form of pasta.

All this lovely liquid for stock or soup will have been made from leftovers at almost no cost, and creating it will have given you great pleasure.

Sauerkraut

Sauerkraut, either from the barrel, tin or jar, may be washed first or used in its saurer state. You can add one or more flavours such as garlic cloves, juniper berries (whole or crushed), caraway seeds, an onion stuck with cloves, fried chopped onion or peppercorns.

When cooking for a long time with pork pieces, bacon pieces, hocks, trotters, game birds, chicken pieces or any other meats lying on top, add a little vinegar, and just a small amount of water, stock or white wine. Surround with peeled potatoes and bake for hours in a low oven. Then, if you like, add, say, pierced frankfurters or Polish ring sausage a little time before taking the dish from the oven.

When cooking sauerkraut as a vegetable, fry chopped onion until brown, add the sauerkraut and some juniper berries, stir around with a fork, cover with stock, and cook very slowly on top of the stove for 2–3 hours.

For a hearty winter stew, fry chopped onion until brown, stirring in a little flour as it colours. Add well-chopped sauerkraut. Then layer this mixture with meat (of almost any kind) in a fireproof pot. Cover with spiced and seasoned, tomato-flavoured stock and cook slowly for around 3 hours on the stove or in a low oven. Tip in a measure of your favourite spirit to enhance this wonderful dish. It will be even better when heated again, and again.

The Dutch like to mix cooked sauerkraut with hot mashed potato as a vegetable. Balls of this mixture, baked dry (unbasted) in the oven with the roast, are excellent.

You will need:

Sauerkraut
Fragrant herbs, spices, and seeds
Pepper and salt
Vinegar
Stock, tomato purée, wine, sometimes spirits
Meats that enjoy being cooked slowly for a long time
Mashed potato for Dutch style

Ways and Methods
One or Two Useful Tips

To Rejuvenate Nuts

If you have nuts that are tired and stale, help is at hand in the form of a frying pan, olive oil and salt.

Heat up only a very little oil in the pan. Toss in the shelled nuts, and, with the heat fairly high, shake the pan and turn the nuts over with a wooden spoon. They will soon be coated with the oil and then begin to roast. Keep them moving in the pan or they will catch and burn. The smell, crackle and possibly smoke (and experience) will tell you when they have roasted enough. Add salt. Turn off the heat and keep stirring for a while as the nuts cool down.

Newly-bought untreated almonds and peanuts can also be roasted in this way.

Tired Coffee

If your (real) coffee has been lying around for some time and lost its freshness, put it into a saucepan and toss it around over a high heat until you can smell it roasting. You find it refreshed and rejuvenated.

Unwanted Smells

The wonderful smell obtained from roasting 'tired coffee' (see p 208) will obliterate unwelcome cooking smells when guests are about to appear for dinner. A dessertspoonful will be enough to roast. Carry the smoking pan around the rooms to be 'scented'.

Emergency Enhancement

Has that stew turned out to be a bit too dry? Are those grated, sliced or chopped vegetables a little tired? Does that sauce need zipping up? Then put some plain yoghurt into a bowl and stir in a little crushed garlic. Add a spoonful or two to the unsuccessful dish and put the remainder in a pleasing bowl on the table so that people can help themselves to more.

YOU WILL NEED:

Yoghurt
Garlic

Olives at all Times

Buy olives of your choice. Those bought with stones in have more taste, and Kalamatas, from Greece, are among the best of the black olives.

Drain the olives and put them into a jar with an airtight lid. Add some extra virgin olive oil and turn the jar around until the olives are coated. Top up the jar with a fresh supply of olives and oil when necessary. The height of oil should be kept at about a quarter of the way up the jar. It is essential to turn the olive jars upside down every few days to keep the contents coated with oil, which in time will become thick, opaque and flavoursome, and will greatly improve the taste of the olives.

In a separate jar you could make a spicy edition with black and green olives adding crushed garlic, a slice or two of de-pipped lemon (or orange) with its peel, crushed coriander seeds and perhaps a dried herb such as thyme.

Olives treated this way are delicious with drinks, or at the table to whet the appetite at the start of a meal.

YOU WILL NEED:	SPICY EDITION:
Olives	Garlic
Olive oil	Lemon (or orange)
	Coriander seeds
	Thyme (optional)

Boiling Waters

Before you throw away the water in which you have boiled pasta or vegetables, consider that it could be the start of a soup, or the dilutant for one. It is a pity to waste excellent liquid like this by throwing it down the drain.

Ice

To make clear ice that chimes in the glass, gently (to avoid adding too many bubbles that will cloud it) fill stout, lidded plastic boxes three-quarters full with tap or boiled kettle water. Deep-freeze them. (Using the ice compartment of a refrigerator will not produce the desired results.)

When frozen, force out the blocks of ice that will now be clear around the sides and cloudy in the middle. Chip sections off the clear edges with an ice pick, oyster opener or pointed corner of a meat-axe blade. This is best done by stabbing the ice in lines until strips break away. Chip these into small cubes. Discard the cloudy centre.

'I always have water with my meal'

Breadcrumbs

Home-made toasted breadcrumbs are far better than those bought in the shops.

When the oven is on, put slices of white or wholemeal bread in a baking tin. Keep the pieces apart from each other. If crowded, turn them over when partly dried, separate them, and allow the heat to reach all parts evenly. They will be ready when crisp, brittle and deep golden brown all over.

You can use a liquidizer for turning these slices into crumbs, but it is not always the easy way, nor is it as satisfactory as using a pestle and mortar. With the latter method it is possible to produce crumbs of a higher quality – crunchy rather than smooth, and it doesn't take very long. Store unwanted crumbs in an airtight jar.

To make soft breadcrumbs for say bread sauce (p. 72) and stuffings, take a white loaf that is at least a day old, cut off the crusts and, in a large bowl, rub the 'crumb' between the fingers to form breadcrumbs. These will keep in the deep freeze for a long time.

English Mustard

English mustard made at home is far superior (and hotter) to that already prepared, and is much under used. Make up your own with powder and water and use to enhance the taste of many a meat or cheese dish.

A day or so after you've mixed your mustard a hard crust will form on the surface. Soften this by pouring water into the mustard pot. Within a few hours the mustard can be used for cooking, or mixed with herbs or breadcrumbs to make a coating for meat to be roasted or grilled.

'Orange Juice' Improvement

'Pure' orange juice, bought in supermarkets and shops in plastic or glass containers, is time-saving and convenient, but unsatisfactory because of the methods used to obtain and transport it. However, by adding the juice of a freshly-squeezed orange, you will make the bought variety taste almost like the real thing.

Charcoaling

There is no doubt in my mind that a domed, enclosed variety of barbecue, such as a Weber, is the best, if expensive. It has the advantages of being able to stay outside permanently, to be used in all weathers, in all seasons, to be precisely controlled, and to be a smoker/charcoaler as well, let alone used as an open grill.

To make sure that you have exact control over the amount of draught entering the lower vents, proceed as follows:

When the machine is empty, apply vertical, white, paint lines to the lower section of the cooker to show where the draught lever should be positioned for fully open and completely closed.

Instructions will say that the coals should not be ignited with methylated spirit – and rightly so, as much can go drastically wrong. Use lump-wood charcoal or briquettes. I use lump wood. Remember that recently-made charcoal will ignite more easily.

First ensure that the lower vent holes of your barbecue are open by riddling any ash out into the tray beneath. Place the grid in position over the charcoal and, with the hood off, set alight. When the charcoal is beginning to burn, put on the hood with the vents above and below fully open for maximum draught – until the charcoal is burning well. Then, through experience, adjust the lower vents, add the food to be cooked and time it to your taste. Wind direction and velocity will have a bearing on this timing.

Slow cooking, with the lower openings almost closed, is often the most satisfactory – for instance, allow 2 hours or so for a good joint of beef.

To smoke and charcoal, place a little, dry, aromatic wood (such as apple or vine) around the edges of the charcoal layer. These will smoulder during the cooking process and impart extra flavour to the food.

Immediately the food has been extracted from the cooker, close both top and bottom vents (you may need a weight on the top, too), then most of the charcoal will be there to use again.

Wine

There are absolutely no fixed rules concerning what wine should accompany a specific dish. NONE.

However, in general terms, the more robust and meaty the dish, the more powerful a red wine could be chosen for it. Accordingly, should the food on offer be vegetable, light-coloured meat or fish, then a white wine might be your choice. Because of the metallic taste sometimes left in the mouth by red wine when drunk with oily fish, many select a white, although the French are quite happy with red. It's all a matter of personal taste.

If there is a wine that you really enjoy, it will probably go perfectly well with whatever you have prepared for the table. There is really no need to search the wine shops or supermarkets for some specific bottle that has been recommended. Choose what you do like – not what you should like.

Fashions in wine change. These are brought about more often than not by considerations of cost. Successful winemakers, districts or countries can easily become greedy, charge too much and lose their regular customers. We can all have a hand in keeping the price of wine low by being both imaginative and selective. The shelves are loaded with wines from around the world. We are lucky to have such a choice.

Several different bottles of wine open on the table at a party offer choice and a subject for discussion. To ask people to pour their own makes good sense.

So how do you choose with confidence? After a long time spent tasting wines, sometimes up to 2000 a year, I have come to certain conclusions. You may disagree with them. Here they are, with brevity, covering the main wine-producing countries of the world.

Australia: Aim for the whites first. These flavoursome wines have the more delicate white Burgundies by the scruff of the neck, and at a far more reasonable price. The reds are powerful, but often lack finesse. The blend of two varieties is sometimes more pleasing than wines made from a single variety. I laid down some

'I bought this bottle of white wine – but when I opened it there was a barbecue going on in there, a festival of fruit with mangos, cherries and limes. I could smell apple blossom and meadows in summertime'

Australian Rhine Riesling for five years. It was bought as a cheap wine. In the intervening years it has acquired exceptionally fine colour and taste.

Balkans: Moderate to good wines appear from all of these countries. The wines from Hungary are improving. Bulgaria has been the star producer and supplier of table wines to the impecunious for many years with their Chardonnays and Cabernet Sauvignons. Merlot is another grape variety that does very well in that country, it may well become the most popular red grape variety here and elsewhere, being soft, easy and fruity. Bulgarian white wines, generally speaking, do not reach the quality of the reds.

England: These white wines have a certain cleanness and floweriness about them. They tend to be expensive. As more vineyards come on stream, suitable grape varieties become established and vinification methods improve, prospects for the future look good. Support this beleaguered industry when possible. Some English wines are delicious.

France: Champagne and Chablis are wines made in unfavourable climates. They are often expensive. Both are far more delicious if given cupboard or cellar time before being consumed. Put some aside for a year or more if it is at all possible. Wine will keep corks moist and airtight if the bottles lie on their sides.

Burgundy is always expensive because of the climate and lack of suitable land available. The price of claret has been rising, but wine prices are cyclical, especially in France when the factors of over-production and greed come into play. Expect a lot from white Burgundy, not so much from white Bordeaux. Sparkling white Burgundy is an excellent buy.

Whites from the Loire are light and pleasing. The sparkling wines from this region are nearly always enjoyable.

Reds from the upper Rhône are often powerful wines and well worth their price.

Generally speaking, if you are unwilling to spend too much on your bottles, aim for the French *Vin de Pays* category for their quality and price.

Vintage dates are not that important for most of us. Producers can make good wine in a bad year and a hash of it in a good one. Then microclimate can enhance or ruin a vintage. However, it is worth noting that ordinary reds are a wise buy after a series of hot summers. Whites are often good after poorer years.

Germany: German producers are strong on wines that are sweet, sweetish and those with a hint of sweetness to them. Nearly all are good value. Dry (Trocken) whites are inclined to be a bit astringent. Wines from the Mosel have great charm and lightness, those from Rheinhessen and the Rheinpfalz more body. Classic, full and fruity wines come from the Rheingau. These are made with juice from the Riesling grape. Liebfraumilch is a very popular blended wine that represents wonderful value for those with a sweeter tooth and not too discerning a nature.

Italy: Italian wines are made for food, just as Italian food is made for wine. This is a very important point to remember. So eat as you drink to obtain the most satisfaction from them. Reds from Piedmont, such as Barolo and the much cheaper Barbera are robust and wonderful for winter dishes. Chianti and especially Montepulciano d'Abruzzo are red wines to swill and enjoy. The Italians are not so good at making classy white wines. But try Orvieto, Galestro and Verdicchio. Asti Spumante, and its almost identical and much cheaper sister Moscato Spumante, are under-rated as sweetish summertime refreshers.

Despite too much unpunished skulduggery in their industry, Italian wines are often wonderful and good value.

The Mediterranean: Sunny, adequate reds are available from Cyprus, Greece, Turkey, Israel, Lebanon, Algeria and Morocco. Château Musar red, from Lebanon, is the star.

Portugal: Portuguese reds are for robust winter meals and will warm the heart. For the best, look for the words *Reserva* and *Garrafeira* on the label. Vinho Verde from the north of the country is a pleasant white wine with a slight prickle to it. Remember that port is a strongly fortified sweet wine (20% alcohol!).

South Africa: Sound and good wines come from South Africa, especially from K.W.V. The standard is high all round for both reds and whites. However, a recently tasted cold-fermented Chenin Blanc from Paarl was a disappointment. The greater number of coloured stripes to be seen on bottle capsules, the better the South Africans believe the wine to be.

South America: Reds, and sometimes whites, especially those from Chile and Argentina, have a good quality/value ratio.

Spain: Woody red Riojas are the stars of Spanish wines. The whites from this region are not nearly as good as the reds, except when aged in cask. Reds and whites from Penedés are often excellent, as are those from Lérida. Sparkling (Cava) wines have plenty of taste and are good value. The rest vary quite a bit. Try Navarra reds for quality and value. Then there are the strong, fortified sherries that range from the bone-dry Manzanillas and Finos to the sweetened Olorosos. These should be more fashionable. Remember their closely related counterparts, the less alcoholic and excellent value Montillas.

USA: Wines to suit all tastes are made throughout the USA. California though, with its star wines from the Sonoma and Napa Valleys, and mass-produced wines from the hot Central Valley, supply the bulk of quality and quantity wine for the American and world markets. Elegant wines from Oregon and Washington State gain ground where class is concerned.

There is no need for most of us to be too serious about wine. Treat it as a normal and very civilized drink– which it is.

Index

Index

Index